Marc Orlando
Training 21st century translators and interpreters:
At the crossroads of practice, research and pedagogy

Transkulturalität – Translation – Transfer, Band 21
Herausgegeben von
Dörte Andres / Martina Behr / Larisa Schippel / Cornelia Zwischenberger

Marc Orlando

Training 21st century translators and interpreters:
At the crossroads of practice, research and pedagogy

Verlag für wissenschaftliche Literatur

Umschlagabbildung: © iStockphoto.com/uschools

ISBN 978-3-7329-0245-3
ISSN 2196-2405

© Frank & Timme GmbH Verlag für wissenschaftliche Literatur
Berlin 2016. Alle Rechte vorbehalten.

Das Werk einschließlich aller Teile ist urheberrechtlich geschützt.
Jede Verwertung außerhalb der engen Grenzen des Urheberrechtsgesetzes ist ohne Zustimmung des Verlags unzulässig und strafbar.
Das gilt insbesondere für Vervielfältigungen, Übersetzungen,
Mikroverfilmungen und die Einspeicherung und Verarbeitung in
elektronischen Systemen.

Herstellung durch Frank & Timme GmbH,
Wittelsbacherstraße 27a, 10707 Berlin.
Printed in Germany.
Gedruckt auf säurefreiem, alterungsbeständigem Papier.

www.frank-timme.de

He who loves practice without theory is like the sailor who boards ship without a rudder and compass and never knows where he may cast.
Leonardo Da Vinci (1452–1519)

Research is research and professional practice is professional practice, and never the twain shall meet?
Daniel Gile (2013)

Acknowledgements

I am, first and foremost, hugely indebted to Professor Dörte Andres, who holds the Chair of Interpreting Studies at the School of FTSK at the University of Mainz in Germersheim, for her enthusiasm, her support and her assistance during the writing of this book. Thank you.

I wish also to express my gratitude to my T&I colleagues at Monash University and, in particular, to Dr Jim Hlavac and Professor Brian Nelson, for their constant support and for having unfailingly shared with me their wealth of knowledge when I worked on my doctoral thesis, the basis for this book.

I am also very thankful to Professor Rita Wilson who, first as the Translation and Interpreting Studies convener, and then as the Head of the School of Languages, Literatures, Cultures and Linguistics at Monash University, has always energetically encouraged me to follow this different research path and to turn my teaching and my T&I professional experience into academic outcomes.

Last but not least, I wish to thank my wife Laurence, and my children Lou, Tom and Lola, simply for being who they are and for giving me both the momentum and the balance that we all need to lead our challenging contemporary lives.

Contents

1 **General introduction** 11
   1.1 Purpose of the book 11
   1.2 Personal background 13
   1.3 Structure of the book 15

2 **T&I practice, training, pedagogy and research** 17
   2.1 T&I practice and training in the 21st century 17
   2.2 Major pedagogical approaches in T&I training 28
   2.3 Translator and interpreter trainers 36

3 **Training *practisearchers* to cross the practice/research divide** 39
   3.1 What divide? 39
   3.2 Origins and development of the vocational/academic dichotomy 48
   3.3 How can the divide be crossed? 54
       3.3.1 Can practice and research inform each other? 55
       3.3.2 The role of research and theory in T&I training 62
             3.3.2.1 Academisation of T&I training 63
             3.3.2.2 Vocational training or academic education? 66
       3.3.3 A student-centred approach to T&I training and education 72
             3.3.3.1 The constructivist approach vs.
                        the instructivist approach 73
             3.3.3.2 Metacognition and T&I training and education ... 76

4 **Future directions** 81
   4.1 Who should train future *practisearchers*? 81
   4.2 Could a practice-informed research approach constitute an acceptable model for academic recognition of T&I practice? 87

5 **Case studies and examples** 93
   5.1 Literary interpreting 94
   5.2 Digital pen technology 100
       5.2.1 Digital pen technology and note-taking training 101

  5.2.2 Digital pen technology and a new hybrid mode of interpreting... 109
  5.2.3 Developments in training, research and in the profession 121
 5.3 Translation process and product-oriented evaluation 124

6 Conclusion 137

Reference list 139

1   General introduction

1.1   Purpose of the book

The objective of this book is to look at the alleged gap between practice and research in Translation and Interpreting (hereafter: T&I) Studies and at the way this gap could be bridged. In particular, the focus will be on the way practice and research can inform each other in the education and training of future translators and interpreters, with a view to training future professionals both as practitioners and researchers in an educational environment that would marry both vocational and academic elements. More precisely, my intent is to investigate relations and synergies between professional T&I practice in different contexts, T&I theory and research and T&I curriculum design in the 21st century. Particular attention will be given to defining the existing divide between practice and research in T&I as well as its origins, and identifying possible ways of bridging this divide. Suggestions will be made concerning ways to undertake research and gain new insights into T&I on the basis of professional practice and experience, as well as to design pedagogical tools for T&I education and training. The aim is to show how these different facets can inform each other in a cyclical manner and to give more prominence to T&I practitioners who wish to turn their practical observations into research that recognises experiential attributes. Outcomes stemming from such an approach will be of interest to the entire T&I community – researchers, practitioners and educators – as it will give more visibility to the profession and will help to bridge the existing gap between practice and research.

Working in a globalised and digitised world, with easy access to new technologies, and having to adapt to many different contexts of work, 21st century translators and interpreters face various challenges. Few would contest the proposition that they should therefore be trained to cope with the new realities of their profession. It is my belief that to meet these challenges and to gain the adaptability necessary to succeed in their role as linguistic mediators who are instrumental for people of different cultures and languages to communicate, today's and tomorrow's professionals should be exposed to, and learn from all dimensions of the translation field: theoretical, technological, practical and professional.

To ensure that trainees are exposed to these contemporary realities, educators in T&I Studies should be kept aware of the changes and requirements in their industry and find ways of bringing them into the classroom to prepare future professionals adequately. This presupposes that these educators have a foot still solidly planted in the practice camp and not merely in the didactics or research one. At the same time, educators and practitioners can no longer ignore the findings of recent and current research in T&I Studies. As an academic discipline, T&I Studies has grown very quickly in the last three decades and produced a quantity of fruitful research which, however, does not always obviously respond to professional challenges or is perhaps not perceived as useful by practitioners or by some educators. The present work is an attempt to reconcile these different fields or contexts, and to propose that T&I educators must aspire to become practitioners-researchers themselves. The argument and the examples provided aim to 'cross the divide' (Shlesinger 2009) between T&I practitioners and researchers and, through various pedagogical approaches, to bring the best of each world back into the T&I classroom.

The purpose will therefore be to show how these various pedagogical, theoretical and professional dimensions can be implemented together in the education and training of professional translators and interpreters. As far as training is concerned, my belief is that trainees should be exposed to both academic and practical knowledge dispensed by both academics and professionals, and along clear and pertinent didactic lines. For many years, when the training of translators and interpreters was touched upon, the question whether it should be led by practitioners or by academics and/or language teachers was crucial (Kelly 2005; Gouadec 2007) and the answer was often lost in the divide between these different worlds. After years of reflection on the profession and on the question of training, and thanks to fruitful research, the prevailing answer is that a necessary interrelationship exists (Gile 1995a; Kearns 2008; Kelly 2005; Pöchhacker 2010). Today, when I consider the fields of translation and interpreting pedagogy, academic research and professional practice through the lens of my own professional experience, I realise that the interaction and correlation between them is an asset that may be used to improve the training of future professional translators and interpreters. There is little doubt in my mind that practice informs research, research informs practice, and findings from both worlds inform training and education. However, as some practitioners and researchers have noted (Chesterman & Wagner 2002; Kearns 2008; Shlesinger 2009), the links between these different aspects of the field are not always clearly established and the academic vs. vocational dichotomy still prevails. Many practitioners are sceptical towards the usefulness of research, or are critical of the prevalence of theory in courses with no obvious applicability to practice, despite the fact that many researchers in the field were at one time practitioners (Katan 2009; Pym & Torres-Simon 2014). This gap between practice and research may be due to the perception that practitioners have of academics and their work. Many professionals may be strangers to the very nature of academic work according to specific research models. As Chesterman (2002) suggests, this situation could change if more practitioners wrote about their practice. I wish to argue that the gap may be bridged if recognised research tools and opportunities were made available to those professionals who would like to write about their experience and perhaps become involved in research activities.

The following questions will guide me in addressing this topic and proposing ways of crossing the divide between both sides of the T&I fence: How can practice and knowledge of the professional world inform research and, similarly, how can research shed light on best practices and professional competence? How can both experiential and theoretical assumptions and observations be applied in the pedagogy of T&I training and education? And finally, how can a practice-informed approach be proposed as an acceptable model to be used to link practice and research in T&I Studies and to implement pedagogical tools responsive to both academic and professional demands?

1.2 Personal background

After nearly twenty years teaching and designing curricula in France, New Zealand and Australia, training language teachers as well as future professional translators and interpreters, working as a freelance conference interpreter and translator, and conducting academic research in T&I studies, I am convinced that the experience and knowledge gained in each field directly informs the other fields. To define the professional I am (a T&I practitioner, educator and researcher), one would need to consider these experiences as a whole. At the same time, what also motivated me to undertake research on the very topic discussed here was the fact that these various facets of my professional personality were often seen and presented as compartmentalised and almost mutually exclusive entities. For people around me, and in my own view as well for some time, I was either a language teacher and teacher trainer/educator, well-trained in the French *didactique des langues* tradition to design curricula according to clear and specific pedagogical projects, sequences and methodologies; or an experienced and recognised professional translator and conference interpreter; or an early career researcher learning how to carry out research in T&I Studies in higher education. But these different facets of my fragmented professional identity were always kept separate and never found a way to merge. It was only years ago, when I was asked to redesign the curriculum for a masters' degree in T&I, that I started putting forward the idea that the inter-disciplinary, multi-faceted knowledge that I had acquired could be capitalised on if the course and pedagogical activities could be restructured around it. For any topic about which I had gained knowledge – whether theoretical or practical – or for any question that would come to my mind after a professional assignment or an academic seminar, I would try to put together, to analyse and to study different views, and to develop training activities that would reflect both sides. Whether it was about translation evaluation and assessment, note-taking techniques in consecutive interpreting, intervention and position in translation, interaction in healthcare interpreting, or time lag management in simultaneous interpreting (to name just a few), the idea was to bring together my own experience (and that of other practitioners-colleagues I was working with) and academic perspectives on the same topic, and to try to design implementable training activities which would take into consideration and reflect all those views and be useful in preparing future professionals. My idea was to combine practice and theory along efficient and common didactic lines.

As an educationalist and trainer with experience in different contexts, institutions and countries, I have always taught according to the principle that (vocational) training should naturally prepare future professionals adequately for the realities of their industry. But I have also developed the firm belief that, to a certain extent, the role of any teacher or educator is to design the curriculum, the teaching activities and the evaluation criteria, with a view to effecting, as the ultimate stage of training, his or her own 'disappearance'. Elaborating on Barthes' idea that the birth of a reader requires the death of the author ('la naissance du lecteur doit se payer de la mort de l'auteur', 1968, p. 63), I would see the gradual symbolic death of the instructor and the birth and emancipation of an independent individual as the objective of any learning process. Curriculum activities should aim at emancipating trainees and at facilitating their acquisition of strong methods and methodologies, and make the instructor's presence superfluous. To do so, I believe that T&I curricula should follow a constructivist approach and be centred chiefly on the learner/student and take into account problem-solving strategies and metacognitive approaches whereby trainees are given the right academic tools to learn how to reflect on their own practice and learning, or 'learn how to learn'. And ultimately, learn how to practice. However, this does not necessarily mean that teacher-centred approaches should be entirely rejected. As also suggested by Westwood (2008), my belief is that training according to a constructivist approach may be optimised if the learner-centred approach is actually implemented in the later stages of the learning and knowledge acquisition process. It has been with this view in mind that I have often designed and proposed T&I pedagogical activities that would integrate practical and theoretical elements and equip future professionals with the ability to respond to the needs of their profession.

1.3 Structure of the book

In the first chapters of this book, I will deal with general questions concerning T&I practice in the 21st century, as well as propose a broad overview of T&I pedagogy. I will also try to define the gap between T&I practice and research, to determine the origins of the vocational/academic dichotomy, and to present suggestions for bridging this gap. I will specifically discuss the role of research and theory in T&I training, the notions of learner-centred vs. teacher-centred approaches in teaching, as well as the concept of the practitioner-researcher, or *practisearcher* (Gile 1995), to be considered as a means of crossing the divide between practice and research. Finally, I will also focus on future directions, especially on discussions about the training of the trainers in T&I and on the practice-led/practice-informed research approach.

The last chapter of the book will aim at presenting case studies and examples of pedagogical activities or research projects which illustrate the argument proposed in this book insofar as they represent initiatives suggesting a natural pathway from either practice and/or research into education and training.

2 T&I practice, training, pedagogy and research

2.1 T&I practice and training in the 21st century

Before discussing further the elements mentioned in the introduction, I believe a snapshot of the T&I professional world as it is today should be provided. The world in which translators and interpreters operate today is immensely different to that of the 1980s or 1990s. Economic, societal and technological changes have affected both practice and training in recent decades.

Market growth and growth in demand and reach in the T&I field have been evidenced in various surveys (Kelly et al. 2010; Drugan 2013). Even if growth figures are difficult to establish and compare globally, Drugan reports that surveys show that the average annual growth of the language service provision (LSP) sector between 1950 and 2004 (5%) was higher than that of international trade (4%). She also notes (2013, p. 9):

> From US $9 billion in 2006, the market for outsourced language services grew by one-third in a single year, reaching US $12 billion by 2007, and further compound annual growth rate of 14.6 per cent between 2008 and 2012 [was predicted]. The largest recent European study estimated annual compound rate at 10 per cent minimum from 2009–15, giving a European language industry valued at a conservative 16.5 billion € by 2015, with the real value likely to be above 20 billion €. […]

According to the survey undertaken by Kelly, Stewart and Hedge (2010), the global language services industry was worth more than US$26 billion in 2010. The *Annual Review of the Translation, Localization, and Interpreting Services and Technology Industry* carried out every year by Common Sense Advisory analysts report that the language services market and the translation industry have continued to grow in complexity and extension because of an apparently ongoing global demand for information sharing (CSA 2014/2015). The industry is estimated to be worth over US$33 billion globally, with experts predicting it could reach $40 billion by 2018. Such predictions have also an impact on the T&I career outlook. For example, the US Bureau of Labor Statistics predicts a 46% job growth in this industry between 2012 and 2022, compared with an average 11% growth for all other careers (US BLS, 2015). These large-scale studies have also shown that the sector is not affected by economic downturns. The reasons for such changes and for the current situation of this industry are multiple and I do not intend to draw up an exhaustive list of them, but two main causes of these changes can be delineated: the globalisation and technologisation of our contemporary world.

With globalisation, the circulation of people, goods, services, ideas and cultures (sometimes freely with the internationalisation of the economy in the last two decades, sometimes through forced migration after conflicts or disasters) has resulted in more and more exchanges between people from different regions of the world who, in previous times, would not have been in contact. A globalised world with facilitated communication and exchanges has imposed challenges on populations and governments, and *a fortiori* on the mediators who help them communicate, as more exchanges mean more communication needs. Market growth in translation has been important following the penetration of free- or mixed-market economies across the globe. And despite the widespread use of English as a *lingua franca*, or of global English, this has driven a higher demand for translation, particularly since the opening of huge new markets in Eastern Europe, Russia, Brazil, India and China since the early 1990s (Drugan 2013). Most high level communication needs (e.g. data reports, business contracts, international meetings) or migration-related services (immigration and community-related assignments) require the services of professional communicators with sound linguistic and cultural skills: translators and interpreters. Both globalisation and increased migration flows have also led to higher volumes of translation. For example, international cooperation in fields like drug or people trafficking, immigration, counter-terrorism, or peacekeeping, have led in particular to the growth of international multilingual organisations which need translators and interpreters to communicate with various countries and to hold their meetings. In 1909, the world had 37 intergovernmental and 176 nongovernmental international organisations; by 1989, there were 300 and 4,200 respectively (Cronin 2003, p. 109). The scope of the work of these organisations has also broadened due to global needs of collaboration in areas like environmental and ecosystems protection and conservation, natural resources exploitation and renewable energies development, climate change management, etc.

Through its technologisation, the world has been affected or altered by technological advances. The use of the Internet, of personal computers and mobiles, has led to a high demand and a growing need for internationalisation, localisation and translation. Multinational companies selling a variety of technological products also explain the growth. 'Wider availability of complex products has meant an increase in technical documentation (games, apps, software)' that require to be translated into many languages worldwide (Drugan 2013, p. 10). Translation volumes have also grown due to the way international business is conducted: anyone involved in business globally needs to stay informed of developments in markets and therefore requires translated information round the clock.

In terms of reach, one might wonder why translations are needed in more languages given that in a globalised world more and more people understand and use English on a daily basis. This change comes in part from those who spend time on the Internet. Web users often prefer and expect online material to be available in their mother tongue and therefore translated. 'Research has consistently demonstrated that web users are more likely to visit a site, spend longer there and, crucially, buy products when a site is available in their own language' (Drugan 2013, p. 12). Online expansion in Africa, Latin America, Asia and the Middle East in recent years also explains such a development. In many countries in those regions, a larger and larger, wealthier and wealthier middle class gets access to commercial and tourism products online. These new web buyers are more likely to 'consume' from their digital devices and computers if the sites and platforms they visit are multilingual. As for the non-commercial sector, the rise in translation needs can be explained by the fact that as the number of international multilingual organisations has grown, their membership has grown too, and the need for more language combinations has followed this trend.

Other developments that might have affected translation reach are the trend towards the protection of culture, and therefore of languages, and the increased visibility of translations. This protective urge may be motivated by a desire to counter the fear that the English language will dominate global communication. As Drugan notes, 'irrespective to the use of the English language as *lingua franca*, a further development is also becoming apparent – the protection of cultures and languages. The translation market will without a doubt profit from this tendency'

(2013, p. 14). This is echoed by Pym, who suggests that 'localisation might actively participate in the saving of difference' (2010a, p. 140). As far as translation visibility is concerned, many factors may have contributed to increased awareness of its existence. With facilitated communication and transport, the availability of the Internet, the global reach of media, the lowering of international trade barriers, and greater travel opportunities, many people have been exposed to a multilingual and multicultural world, especially in monolingual countries. And this has promoted translation in its various forms. Even anti-globalisation movements, by mobilising activists and disseminating their arguments at local, regional and global levels, have contributed to an increased awareness of translation.

In all cases, these multiple changes have substantially affected the way professional translators and interpreters work, and they cannot be ignored by the profession. For all 21st century T&I practitioners, adaptability is a key element. Today's professionals have to know about the different norms and standards proper to the various markets in which they work, whether local or global. They have to accept to work in different contexts and environments. For example, in the 20th century, professional translators and interpreters would often work in-house in their companies' translation departments. Today, this is rare. The majority of the professionals are freelancers who work directly for clients or language service providers, and are in direct competition with practitioners from all over the world. Pym et al.'s report on the status of the translation profession in the European Union (2012) shows that the proportion of freelancers in the profession 'would generally appear to have grown since the 1990s, when many large companies took to outsourcing their translation demands' (2012, p. 88) and that the average proportion of freelancers globally is around 78%, ranging from 50% in China to 89% in the UK.

Professionals also have to accept that their geographical region is not their only area of work. Translators in the 21st century can work for agencies or clients from various parts of the world (Katan 2009; Pym et al. 2012). Today translation services operations are managed 24/7 by shifts from different platforms based in different parts of the globe. Different time zones are no longer a problem but can become an asset when the deadlines to submit a translated piece are getting stricter and shorter. Translators of the 21st century can be based more or less where they want provided they have an Internet connection and a computer at hand. Thanks to new digital technology and videoconference facilities, interpreters can also be asked to interpret remotely, provided acceptable working conditions are respected. Practitioners of the 21st century have become translators and interpreters without borders.

Practitioners constantly have to upgrade their skills if they want to remain competitive in their markets. But beyond linguistic and cultural skills and competence, professionals must also be able to respond to technological challenges, bearing in mind that these challenges are constantly changing. As Gouadec (2007, p. 336) puts it: 'Each technological generation is now thought to last no more than four years.' Like many other professions, translators and interpreters have had to learn to work differently since the introduction into their world of all sorts of digital technology tools. The appearance of software programmes, Computer Assisted Translation tools (CAT tools), Translation Memory (TM) and Machine Translation, to name just a few, has forced translators to change their ways of translating and to adapt to the new expectations and requirements of their clients. As reported by Drugan (2013, p. 17), technological developments have had an impact on delivery and return in the industry. Deadlines, content, output volume, speed and rates have been affected by a move from paper dictionaries and handwritten translations to photocopiers and fax machines in the 1990s, and then to today's personal computers and laptops, fast Internet connections, software and electronic tools. 'The Internet Age has brought a change in translation speed more significant than any that went before. […] Entirely new challenges affect translation deadlines' (Drugan 2013, p. 18), as well as content and daily outputs, which are important elements to consider when one wishes to measure a translator's productivity. There is also a positive side to these technological developments: as noted above, they have generated more work for translators and also more tools to help them to increase their productivity. However, the obvious consequence is that 'professional translators in developed countries are unlikely to survive without PCs, email, search engines and word processing' (Drugan 2013, p. 23). As for interpreters, the technological age has also had an impact on their activity. New technologies make it possible for them to work remotely (through video or phone, for example) (Braun 2007; Napier 2011; Ozolins 2011), to use different equipment (portable wireless equipment), or to work in different modes of interpreting (digital recorders or digital pen technology in the consecutive-simultaneous mode) (Orlando 2010b, 2014, 2015; Pöchhacker 2004). Some technologies, such as those enabling speech to text conversion, or the conversion of written input into spoken output, could even make them redundant. This has obvious consequences in terms of their need to be adaptable and open to new practices if they want to remain competitive and employable (Moser-Mercer 2005), and will inevitably change their working conditions in the years to come, 'with issues such as stress, visual access and psycho-social factors requiring particular attention' (Pöchhacker 2004, p. 201).

In the 21st century, the scope of activities for translators is much broader than it used to be. They obviously translate various text types (technical, legal, medical, financial, literary, cultural, media) but they also use translation software and information technology, revise translations, post-edit texts translated with machine translation, summarise texts, edit and adapt both originals and translations, do technical writing, manage projects, train peers, subtitle and dub multimedia texts, work on localisation teams, create translation memories and terminology databases within commercial translation software, do research in computational linguistics, machine translation and language engineering. Translators are expected to respond to industry needs and cover a broad range of tasks (Gouadec 2007; Katan 2009; Pym et al. 2012). Using data from a 2005 survey of more than a 100 employers, Gouadec (2007, p. 329) lists the employers' expectations of translators' attributes as follows, in order of importance: language skills; knowledge of specific translation tools; qualifications in T&I; knowledge of quality control procedures; revision and terminology management; project management; ability to handle non-standard translations; IT and software localisation skills; experience.

For interpreters, too, the scope of aptitudes and contexts of work has broadened. Even if they specialise more than translators (Katan 2009a, p. 192), they may not be as compartmentalised as they used to be and often have to interpret in various contexts and in various modes, onsite or remotely. They can work as permanent staff or freelancers for institutions (UN, European Commission, European

Parliament, international organisations); for conferences and international meetings; on business or diplomacy assignments; as community interpreters in various fields (immigration, health, court, legal, police, education, refugee tribunals...) and subfields; in the media; in conflict and disaster zones; in refugee camps, etc. Freelance interpreters today can be asked to work and offer their services in many areas, and their assignments may in many cases encompass different fields and contexts of work.

The status of T&I professionals has evolved as well in recent decades. However, the way they are perceived and the way they perceive themselves have not always been well-defined. In 2008, in order to clarify the status of T&I professionals and to determine if their activity is an 'occupation' or a 'profession', Katan carried out an online survey amongst them.

> The questionnaire focused on translator and interpreter perception of their working world, their mindset, and the impact of Translation Studies and university training on that world. Nearly 1000 respondents replied to the questionnaire worldwide. Particular questions focused on how translation should be taught, the role and status of the profession (ideally and in practice), and on personal satisfaction. The results show that university training has had little impact, and that this group of respondents have relatively little interest in the university itself in comparison with lifelong learning, with most emphasis placed on practice and self-development. (Katan 2009a, p. 187)

I will discuss further some of the results of the survey which are relevant to the practice-theory divide and training, but it is interesting to note at this point that to the question 'what makes T/I a profession?' 67% of respondents answered that skills, competence and expertise achieve this, 25% answered that training does, and only 2% thought that the theory of the discipline does. Despite the fact that respondents did not show much interest in university training or in the theory of the discipline, a quarter of them believed that training is what makes T&I a profession and is important, regardless of whether it is academic or professional, and that experience and life-long learning should also be recognised and valued (Katan 2009a, p. 193).

One of the main concerns of the profession in terms of status is that it is an unregulated profession and nearly anyone can call him/herself a *translator*. As reported by Pym et al. (2012, p. 20):

> In no country that we have surveyed is any academic qualification – or indeed any kind of formal qualification at all – required in order to use the term 'translator' or its equivalent *generic* terms. Almost anyone at all can be called a 'translator'. More technically, the general title of 'translator' is virtually unprotected.

Moreover, their report shows that public employers like governments or international organisations generally prefer candidates who have completed a degree in T&I, but technically and legally do not ask for any specialised qualification in T&I to work as a translator (2012, p. 22). Even if this situation has existed for a long time, one would assume that, given the complexities of the profession today, specific T&I training will now be a requirement for anyone starting in the profession.

Because of the new professional demands and expectations (daily output, technological and geographical requirements), and of changes and shifts in the profession, the 21st century T&I practitioner is subjected to pressures that her/his predecessors would not have known. Logically, such changes and shifts have had an impact on the way future professionals need to be trained. And training contexts are also different today to what they used to be a few decades ago (Hurtado Albir 2007). As Gouadec puts it, the idea that translators are trained on the job is not sustainable, as there are 'not enough spontaneously generated translators around to meet market demands' (2007, p. 327). Training is therefore necessary, and there have never been as many university courses and programmes in translation as there are today. But this brings challenges for training institutions, as it is 'absurd to pretend that anyone who has graduated with a degree in translation will necessarily make a good translator' (Gouadec 2007, p.327). There seems to be agreement that there is indeed a need to train translators to meet existing demand and to face rising volumes in the future (Gouadec 2007; Katan 2009), but there should also be agreement on the need to train 'good' translators and to train them 'well'.

With regard to T&I training, it is relevant to mention that globalisation and market needs also have an impact on geographical locations of courses and the types of training to be developed in those locations. As identified by Gouadec (2007, p. 330), there are two types of countries:

> Those where there is a real dearth of properly trained specialised professional translators (i.e. China, Cambodia, Brazil, South Africa, Turkey, Mozambique…) and where there is a vital need for translator training courses in the national languages; and those where the question is mainly training those who will take over from the outgoing generation of translators and who will be able to meet the new market needs and challenges.

Without counting vocational diplomas, which do not lead to postgraduate education and do not include (or contain very little) theoretical content, training and education of T&I professionals is today provided mainly at universities. Masters programmes have mushroomed all over the world. In the past, when they received training, future T&I professionals were trained within T&I schools (based mainly in Europe – Geneva, Heidelberg, Paris, Trieste, Vienna (Pöchhacker 2004, p. 31); but now, with multiple changes in the academic world, these schools have been absorbed into broader faculties and universities. Even if their curricula remain to a certain extent the same, they have been turned into masters degrees designed according to new qualification frameworks, appropriate to the country in which they are based (Pöchhacker 2004, p.179). The academic nature of studies has also imposed another shift on such a specialised training: it is no longer only vocational and some research activities in the discipline will have to be undertaken by any T&I student. Because – and thanks to – such changes, the nature of studies in T&I has changed and is not focussed only on professional competence and skills. Research activities which complement the more practical elements of the training help students and staff to theorise and conceptualise some aspects of the profession. Students in T&I Studies today are much more exposed to theory and research in their field than T&I students of the past. This academisation of T&I training will be discussed in greater detail a bit later.

One issue related to the increasing number of training programmes is the relevance of the training content. Too many graduates do not find employment and too many employers or companies do not find the right translator, 'suitable' for the jobs or contracts (Gouadec, 2007). This raises the question of course objectives, which I will discuss further together with other issues related to T&I

training. The multiplication of training programmes worldwide has induced researchers, trainers and educators, in collaboration with the professional associations and representatives of T&I employers or institutions that hire translators and interpreters, to develop benchmarks and recognisable labels to ensure that the right and necessary aptitudes and skills are taught in the course of studies, and to differentiate and classify masters' degrees and postgraduate courses offered in T&I. It is in this context that frameworks and labels like the European Master in Translation (EMT) or the European Master in Conference Interpreting (EMCI) have been developed for European programmes in T&I to apply for, to show how they comply with standardised training and research norms. The EMT project, for example, was established as 'a quality label for university translation programmes that meet agreed professional standards and market demands' in order 'to improve the quality of translator training' (EMT website, 2014). The EMCI is 'a programme designed to equip young graduates with the professional skills and knowledge required for conference interpreting. It seeks to meet the demand for highly-qualified conference interpreters, in the area of both widely and the less widely-used and less-taught languages' (EMCI website, 2014).

It is also to respond to this need to benchmark excellence in training and research in university T&I programmes that an association such as CIUTI (The Conférence Internationale permanente d'Instituts Universitaires de Traducteurs et Interprètes), which was formed in the early 1960s as a select group of T&I recognised institutions, has broadened and diversified its membership to reach a more global audience and to recognise that high-level training and education in T&I exist in various parts of the world and contexts of work. The 'membership requires fulfilment of strict quality criteria and is a distinct seal of quality', as the CIUTI website states, and the association is 'devoted to excellence in T&I training and research, [and] being a member of the CIUTI family is both a rewarding status and a continuous challenge in the light of changing market needs and ongoing research' (CIUTI website, 2014).

As a consequence of the growing numbers of translators worldwide, and of the growing number of technologies being developed to increase the daily output of professionals, implying growing variability in the quality of translation works, many service providers have developed quality control (QC) or quality assurance

(QA) procedures, and many professional associations or governments are aiming to develop T&I credentialing or certification systems (Chen 2009; Hlavac 2013; Mikkelson 2013; Stejskal 2005). Such systems and procedures would also help to classify or filter professionals, no longer on the basis of their degree alone but also on the basis of professional accomplishments and credentials. They would also set standards of competence and ensure clients of quality services (Mikkelson 2013). As reported by Gouadec, there has been an ongoing debate in the profession over the question of course validation and the way translation courses are recognised and qualifications delivered which 'echoes the struggle undertaken by some who would like to protect the profession by requesting that anyone wanting to practise as a professional translator should have to prove that they can meet certain minimum standards' (2007, p. 347). For me, such an aspiration to protect the profession for quality assurance and to ensure that those working as professionals are well trained to do so is perfectly legitimate as long as the expected quality control takes into account the various facets and stakeholders of the profession. I also believe that adjusting the T&I training courses to professional requirements can be done only if the representatives of the profession, the industry and academics work together so that effective professional quality control and certification can be established (Mikkelson 2013). To illustrate this trend towards developing certifications and standardisation, one could mention the development of a Trans-European certification system in Europe (2013–2014) that is likely to contain testing requirements (Centre for Translation Studies University of Vienna 2013). This EU-funded project, most commonly known as 'TransCert', is based at the Centre for Translation Studies, University of Vienna, but also includes stakeholders from other European universities and other relevant organisations. Of relevance too, is the International Organisation for Standardisation (ISO) which recently developed ISO 17100:2015, providing requirements for the core processes, resources, and other aspects necessary for the delivery of a quality translation service that meets applicable specifications. Its other recently adopted document with guidelines for community interpreting contained in ISO 13611:2014 provides criteria and recommendations for oral and signed interpretation during community assignments. It also contains scope for testing of certain skills amongst candidates and the recognition of certification from accredited government bodies that conduct tests to award certification in (community) interpreting (ISO 2014). AIIC, the international association of conference interpreters, has also joined this project in order to create a sub-committee working on standardisation in conference interpreting (Perez-Guarneri & Ziegler, 2013).

Preparing future professionals today requires that training institutions implement a training vision that accounts for the above-mentioned changes in the profession. For example, and as explained by Drugan, given the industry focus on processes and quality levels, translator education could largely contribute to quality-related issues in training (2013, p. 185). However, the fact that institutions could put mechanisms in place to identify changes and new challenges in the profession and try to raise awareness about them is not sufficient. They also would have the responsibility to provide training and education along recognised pedagogical lines and to expose trainees to theory and research that could be of use when applied to their competence and skills. The increasing role of technology in the profession will impact on T&I training, and training institutions have to introduce all sorts of equipment to meet the requirement of the profession. There is also a need to engage students in authentic tasks mirroring and taking into account the demands and norms of the industry, bearing in mind the fact that the rapid changes observed seriously challenge the primacy of universities. Lambert (1976) wondered if universities 'are flexible enough to account for systematic and rapid changes' and concluded that 'in our contemporary world, we need new models for observation, analysis, action – and teaching' (cited in Drugan 2013, p. 185). I agree with this view, even four decades later. Indeed, it is not by using only training methods and methodologies from the 20th century that we will train 21st century professionals and respond efficiently to today's needs. Innovation and creativity are needed in T&I Studies today. I am not the first and will surely not be the last to make such a plea (see for example Echeverri 2008).

2.2 Major pedagogical approaches in T&I training

Research in T&I Studies and in T&I education has developed quickly and followed various turns in the last decades, and I propose hereafter to provide a general overview of approaches and trends which have marked the pedagogy of the discipline. In order to properly discuss the topic of the academic vs. vocational dichotomy and the way to reduce the gap between T&I practice and theory, it is relevant to consider the way translator and interpreter training has changed in the last decades along various different approaches. I will be looking at translator training first and then at interpreter training.

As discussed by Dorothy Kelly in her *Handbook for Translator Trainers* (2005/2014), one can sum up the history of translator training by pinpointing the following trends and approaches.

For many decades, not to say centuries, the 'teacher-centred transmissionist tradition' (2005, p. 11), which focussed exclusively on the translation product, prevailed in translator training. The rationale was that trainees would learn the skills simply by translating and that a model translation would exist and serve as a benchmark, that of the teacher. In 1980, Delisle proposed a different approach to T&I teaching by underlining the importance of clear and achievable teaching and learning objectives in the curriculum, developed around contrastive-linguistic activities. With clearer objectives, the communication between teachers and students was better and the approach allowed a better choice of teaching tools and more varied learning activities. This view provided a basis in translator training for the assessment of learning. This was followed by Nord's view (1991) that training should simulate professional practice. This gave birth to profession-based learner-centred approaches. Under the umbrella of the functionalist approach, the focus was translation and it was target text oriented, with a more professional and realistic purpose to be achieved in the translation activity. The teaching and learning activities were student-centred and process-oriented, with however 'a considerable teacher intervention' (Kelly 2005, p. 14), especially in the initial stages of training.

Both Delisle (1980) and Nord (1991) stressed the importance of the process of translation, not simply the product, anticipating the work of Gile (1995a), who showed that it is in mastering the process of translation that future professionals gradually acquire professional expertise. Gile's approach was original insofar as it combined for the first time consideration of both translation and interpreting. His view is that both activities are acts of communication and that training should be focussed on the process of translation or of interpretation through various units of activity and combinations of efforts to be managed (Gile 1995a). For him, quality should be seen from the professional point of view; knowledge acquisition ('documentary research') is paramount; and the focus on the process allows faster progress and opens the door to clearer translation strategies, and helps to solve issues in terms of fidelity to the source text or the alleged untranslatability of certain texts. Gile interestingly suggests however that this focus on the process should be limited to the first stage of training and that towards the end a product-oriented approach should prevail (1995a, 2005).

It was also in 1995 that Kiraly proposed an approach in which cognitive and psycholinguistic research could be applied to training. Kiraly's idea was that training should rely on 'a pedagogy based on the accurate theoretical description of translation practice' (1995, p. 3). He carried out research on think-aloud protocols (TAP), for example, and developed the idea that a key aim in training was the development by translators of the awareness of their role: what he called 'the translator's self-concept'. For Kiraly, what would prevail in training would be the acquisition of interlingual, intercultural and intertextual associations; error analysis which would allow better strategies and more translation alternatives, and the translation activity would be envisaged beyond semantic and syntactic correctness. 'Training should reorganise around a theoretical framework that allows the identification of cognitive resources that students should acquire and the pedagogical tools for teaching and testing the acquisition of these skills and knowledge' (1995, p. 112). The study of translation based on cognitive science aiming at an application in training translators led Kiraly to identify clear-cut and exploitable differences between trainees and professionals in different areas, such as the use of dictionaries, their distance from the lexical transfer, their awareness of translation problems, their consideration of macro and micro elements in the translation process, their focus on style, revision and the user's needs, their lack of assuredness when translating out of their mother tongue, and many other interesting aspects to be considered when designing curricular activities.

Another approach developed at that time in the training of translators was the situational approach or 'translation in situation', promoted in the mid-90s by Vienne (1994) or later by Gouadec (2002). For Vienne, the translation class activity should be made up of a series of tasks already carried out by the teachers professionally and which would allow the trainers to become initiators in the process in a more realistic way. The approach is functionalist but Vienne totally rejects the simulation of the professional task, alleging that, in the classroom, it may be too difficult, at times impossible, to carry out a realistic analysis of the situation and to answer the questions which may arise. The method proposed by Vienne was the situational analysis of the translation commission in which the teacher/initiator responds to students' queries and questions, giving them a framework within which to carry out the translation task. The teacher becomes a requester and the student a trainee translator. Gouadec advocated the same project-based approach and type of activities and started incorporating into his curriculum real translation commissions for real clients.

In the attempt to design training activities which improve the translator's competence and prepare the future professional for the industry in which he/she will work, a multitude of approaches have been developed, and it is not my purpose here to cover them all. Pym's 'minimalist' definition of that competence and suggested approach (2003) is however relevant to single out. Pym argued that, because of the numerous and constant changes in the profession, adding new dimensions to translator competence (the use of new technologies, new modes of translating, new media and software, etc.), pedagogical theory of training cannot keep up. He therefore opted for a simple definition of the competence that would define the translational process to be taken into account in training, based on the following twofold competence: 'The ability to generate a series of more than one viable target text (TT1, TT2… TTn) for a pertinent source text; and the ability to select only one viable target text from this series, quickly and with justified confidence' (Pym 2003, p. 489). This notion supports the idea that there is an indivisibility of theoretical and practical knowledge which must be recognised when considering translation competence, as translation is viewed as a process of producing and selecting between hypotheses, a problem-solving process in which the importance of theory becomes clear.

Also pertinent was the task-based approach developed in translator training by Hurtado Albir (1999) and Gonzalez Davies (2004), which had been applied in the teaching and learning of foreign languages since the 1980s. As explained by Kelly, this approach advocates that translation tasks must be 'a chain of activities with the same global aim and a final product' (2005, p. 18) and implies an overall curricular design based on learning outcomes (an application of Biggs' (2000) systematic approach to aligned curriculum). She notes that in a way it is a further development of Delisle's approach according to objectives.

In her panorama of translator training, Kelly also mentions Robinson's student-centred approach (1997/2003) based on a balance between slow academic learning and fast, real-world learning. Central to Robinson's philosophy is the idea that the translator is a life-long learner who learns first from personal experience but can also be helped by other channels: theories, other professionals, etc.

The next key approach is that of Kiraly at the turn of the century (2000). In the book he published that year, Kiraly advocates a socio-constructive approach: a collaborative approach to translator training in which the idea of the self-concept still exists but is associated with the socialisation of the translator in the professional community. The idea in training is to opt for 'a pedagogical event with a highly realistic, and if possible genuine, translation project' (Kelly 2005, p. 18).

Several translator trainers and authors (Kelly 2006; Marco 2004) have since designed curricula borrowing elements and aspects from the last two perspectives.

From the curriculum design point of view, valuable work has been carried out by training or professional associations like CIUTI, or by FIT, the *Fédération Internationale des Traducteurs* (e.g. the FIT POSI project on practice-oriented course content for translators and interpreters initiated in 1996) and is currently underway at the Directorate General for Translation at the European Commission with its European Master's in Translation (EMT) project; similarly Gabr (2003/2007), Kelly (2005), Kearns (2006) and Calvo (2009) deal specifically with curricular design issues as opposed to classroom activities *per se*.

The topic of translator training has long been debated and many attempts have been made to characterise it. The differences in views in translator training are often the result of the different contexts in which training occurs. This is a reason why I have decided to focus on the major approaches which offered a new direction in training, being aware that not all approaches have been outlined or covered here. In reviewing some of these approaches and the attempts to characterise translator training, Kearns (2006, p. 55) points out that:

One prominent feature of these attempts is the extent to which they *are highly* disparate, revealing the training of translators to involve an eclectic array of variables which may be assessed, from teaching methodologies, to academic/vocational ideologies which impinge on training procedures, to the revolutionary impact of technology on the field, to international governmental policy agreements on education, to name just a few.

Such variables, as well as the very different and specific contexts (times, societies, etc.) where training takes place, may well explain why one cannot define *a* translator training model.

As far as interpreter training is concerned, a chronological presentation of the various pedagogical approaches is somehow more difficult to establish, as this area has evolved in a less demarcated way compared to translator training. Following Pöchhacker's presentation of the pedagogy of Interpreting Studies (2004), one can start by pointing out that, since the 1950s, because of the strong belief among trainers that a thorough understanding of what is taught is essential, there have always been important links between practice and training/teaching. One can also note that the research activities conducted in this area since the 1960s have often been carried out to serve interpreter training. All in all, however, it must also be acknowledged that 'as a research topic as such, the pedagogy of interpreting has generated little systematic investigation but a comparatively large body of experiential description' (Pöchhacker 2004, p. 177). Over the years, interpreter training has revolved round the same prominent themes, which include student selection, performance assessment and teaching methods to develop interpreters' core skills and competence. The reflections on curricular issues remained limited until the 1980s and 1990s, 'when the strongly profession-based tradition of (conference) interpreter training was complemented by a scientific, process-oriented approach' (Pöchhacker 2004, p. 177).

For most of the twentieth century interpreter training was carried out with the objective of developing professional skills and competence in the consecutive and simultaneous modes of interpreting, and the first generation of trainers, themselves accomplished professionals, 'established a lasting tradition of training by apprenticeship, that is, transfer of know-how and professional knowledge from master to student, mainly by exercises modelled on real-life tasks' (Pöchhacker

2004, p. 178). This approach could be related to the above-mentioned teacher-centred transmissionist approach to translator training. This apprenticeship approach was supported and reaffirmed by AIIC (the International Association of Conference Interpreters, which was created in 1953 and has always been influential in the area of interpreter training), and was implemented through a 'school policy' adopted by the association in 1959. The interpreter training courses had a professional/vocational profile, were designed and taught by practising conference interpreters, and were offered in institutions with an independent organisational status of schools like those in Geneva, Germersheim, Heidelberg, Paris, Trieste or Vienna (a status often expressed in their designations: *Dolmetscherinstitut* or *Dolmetscherschule, Ecole (Supérieure), Institut Supérieur, Hoger Instituut, Scuola Superiore, Escuela Universitaria*). 'In this institutional context, pioneering professionals produced the first textbooks of interpreting (Herbert 1952; Rozan 1956; Seleskovitch 1968; van Hoof 1962) and interpreting programmes throughout the 1970s and 1980s foregrounded the professional rather than the academic dimension of higher education' (Pöchhacker 2004, p. 31).

The most influential school of thought at that time was the Paris School (ESIT, Paris), whose pedagogical tenet, derived from Danica Seleskovitch's *théorie du sens* (the Interpretive Theory of Translation), was strongly profession-based. The Paris School's paradigm came to be questioned in the 1980s as a more scientific and theory-driven approach to training was called for by several scholars whose training models were developed directly from a more cognitive process-oriented paradigm: the models, for example, of Arjona 1990, Gile 1995, Kalina 1998, Lambert 1988, Moser-Mercer 2000, Riccardi 1996 (Pöchhacker 2004, p. 178). It is from this time that interpreting training shifted towards 'a more theory-friendly curriculum' and interpreter training became more 'academised' (Pöchhacker 2004, p. 31).

There was another shift in the 1990s and 2000s, with a move in interpreter training practices towards a more student-oriented and interaction-oriented refined approach. Emphasis was placed on advances in curricular theory (for example, with Sawyer's work 2004) taking into account scientific approaches as well as personal and social aspects of instruction. This approach has been complemented by various recent technological advances which allow interpreter trainers to examine empirical data in different digital forms and can facilitate the development of pedagogical activities as well as simplifying assessment, feedback and remediation (Lindquist 2005; Orlando 2010b; Winteringham 2010).

Based on observations by Gile (2009a), Pöchhacker (2004), Sawyer (2004) and Setton (2010), it appears that most of the literature on interpreter training shows that teaching activities can be grouped in three categories: consecutive interpreting and note-taking techniques; simultaneous interpreting for international conferences; and dialogue interpreting for community-based situations. As noted by Pöchhacker, over the years the didactic approaches aimed at developing pedagogical activities relevant to these three categories have been either descriptive ('How I teach this skill') or prescriptive ('How this skill should be taught'). They could be summed up by subsets as follows: for consecutive interpreting most activities revolve round active listening and analysis (e.g. Jones 1998), memory exercises, processing overload (e.g. Gile 1995a), note-taking (e.g. Alexieva 1994, Ilg 1996), and public speaking (e.g. Mead 2000). For simultaneous interpreting (e.g. Gillies 2013, Andres & Behr 2015), they are mainly made of dual-tasks/split attention exercises, active listening and analysis, exercises in paraphrasing, coping strategies, focussing on the process instead of the product only, and sight translation/sight interpretation. For dialogue interpreting (e.g. Gentile et al. 1996) the focus is on interpersonal interaction, intercultural communication, turn-taking and role-plays.

An exhaustive list of approaches exceeds the scope of this book, but one cannot present a summary of approaches in translator and interpreter training at university level without mentioning the fact that training occurs also in non-academic settings in the form of workshops or short courses conducted by professional associations or by T&I programmes, as part of continuing education or professional development – what Pöchhacker labels 'meta-level training' (2004, p. 189). This type of training generally aims at improving professional standards or at raising ethical and social awareness amongst T&I professionals and users of T&I professionals, and caters for practitioners, newcomers to the profession, or professionals working in new and emerging communities with minority language for which university training does not exist.

2.3 Translator and interpreter trainers

When considering all the above-mentioned changes in the profession and the training environment, as well as in pedagogy and research, one crucial question to ask is the following: who are T&I trainers and educators who bear the responsibility to prepare future practitioners and make them aware of the realities and norms of their future industry as well as of the relevance of particular professional and academic competences and skills to be developed and acquired? Who has the ability to provide them with what Sawyer called 'the practical skills training' and the 'scholarly acquisition of abstract knowledge' (2004, p. 77), elements he also labelled as 'interpreter training' on the one hand, and 'interpreter education' on the other?

As already discussed, from the 1950s and for a few decades, the main belief was that both translator and interpreter training should be done by practitioners, in a 'transmissionist tradition' (Kelly 2005) or by 'apprenticeship' (Pöchhacker 2004), a teaching act that Kearns also calls 'a teacher-centred *performance magistrale*' (2006, p. 38). Training in T&I schools was done by practicing professionals, and activities generally mirrored real-life situations. In the last 20 years, the profession has become aware of the need for training the trainers and several trainers/researchers have pushed for a move towards training the trainers in T&I, encouraging the development of research models in the discipline (Andres & Behr 2015; Gile 1990; Kelly 2005; Pöchhacker 2002). Despite a certain 'academisation' in T&I training at university level in recent decades (Pöchhacker 2004), professional experience is still seen and often recommended in many programmes as the essential prerequisite for successful teaching (Kelly 2005, p. 55). Many trainers and scholars (e.g. Gouadec 2003; Kiraly 1995) even recommend that professional practice should be carried out simultaneously when teaching in T&I programmes. As a result of this need to cover both vocational and academic knowledge during the training, many T&I training institutions have chosen to employ professional practitioners for the training part – these instructors sharing their experience without paying much attention to research; and academics with knowledge or expertise in T&I Studies – these educators sharing their scholarly knowledge but having no or very limited experience in T&I practice. Nevertheless, several educators (e.g. Gouadec 2007; Sawyer 2004) advocate that training programmes should endeavour to avoid being either too academic or too professionally-oriented. Ideally, they should also attempt not to leave the methodological and theoretical elements to the academics and the professional reality to the professionals. 'Academics should know what professional translation is about and professionals also must get acquainted with the theories and methodologies and models' (Gouadec 2007, p. 350).

Even though the need to cover both the professional and the academic dimensions in training has generally been acknowledged, it has been argued by many that teaching prerequisites cannot be exclusively professional and practical, or exclusively academic, and cannot be only a combination of both either (Hurtado Albir 2007; Kelly 2005; Kiraly 2000; Setton 2010). Being an experienced T&I professional, or a widely published and well-regarded academic, is no guarantee of pedagogical competence and training skills. As Kelly points out, 'those who [teach] should first and foremost be competent trainers' (2005, p. 151). For her, the areas of competence or expertise required for training are professional practice, knowledge of Translation Studies as an academic discipline, and teaching skills, which should be a prerequisite for any type of training role undertaken in an educational context. However, this is unfortunately too often ignored in tertiary institutions. As Kelly insists (2008, p. 102):

> It is paradoxical that universities in many countries have traditionally paid little attention to teacher training. In many countries, compulsory training exists for all other levels of education, but at universities it is simply assumed that those who know know how to teach. It is still the case in many countries that new members of teaching staff are left literally to sink or to swim in the classroom, while more attention is paid, for example, to their training as researchers in their discipline.

This essential question of *who T&I trainers and educators should be* will be further developed later in chapter 4 but, with a view to advocating that developing practice and research essential skills would be a key aspect of T&I training, and that the professional experience of trainers and educators should be promoted and turned into research and pedagogical tools, it is important to recognise that being a practitioner and/or a researcher does not equip one to be a teacher/trainer. Professionals bring precious experience to the classroom, and 'it is certainly enriching for students at translation schools to have professional translators as teachers but this is not without its problems: professional translators lack specific training' (Kelly 2005, p. 55). As far as university lecturers are concerned, their institutions expect them to devote their time to teaching and research activities as well as administrative tasks, but not to develop their teaching and training skills. This undoubtedly has an impact on the way translators and interpreters are trained and, like many other trainers, I argue that training programmes in T&I and teams of instructors are better led by staff members with training and teaching experience and competence, and a good understanding of didactics. I believe it is the responsibility of universities to promote research on professional practice, models and protocols so that their teaching staff members are shown how research can gain from practice, how practice can gain from research, and how these gains can be turned into effective pedagogical tools to be implemented in the curriculum. But, as I will discuss in relation to the vocational/academic dichotomy, there is always the risk that, not wanting to be accused of becoming too vocational, 'universities will shelter behind the cosy walls of academia', and will ensure professionals cannot 'take over translating training altogether on the grounds that "they know best"' (Gouadec 2007, p. 351).

3 Training *practisearchers* to cross the practice/research divide

To develop further the idea that experiential, theoretical and pedagogical knowledge should be considered as complementary parts of the same holistic entity in T&I training, I will now focus on the alleged gap between practice and theory in T&I Studies, try to determine its origins, and make suggestions on how to cross the practice/research divide.

3.1 What divide?

'There can be few professions with such a yawning gap between theory and practice.' It is with this provocative assertion about the translation profession that Emma Wagner and Andrew Chesterman open their 2002 book *Can theory help translators: A dialogue between the ivory tower and the wordface* (p. 1). I too tend to believe that very few people working in this discipline, either on the academic or the professional side, would be surprised to hear of such a gap, or would contest or deny its existence, even though most participants in this profession (practitioners, researchers or educators) tend to agree that practice and practitioners' experience are the main source of research, and that research should somehow be useful to practitioners. The need to reconcile each side and to bridge the gap is sometimes contested (Wadensjö 2011), but not the existence of the gap. So, what is the nature of the gap between practitioners and researchers, between theory and practice in the discipline?

A good example of the way the divide manifests itself can be found in one of the findings of Katan's 2008 survey of about 1,000 T&I professionals, which, as foregrounded earlier, revealed that only 2% amongst them thought that the theory of T&I is useful to define and benefit their profession (Katan 2009a, p. 192). The study also revealed that about 55% of the respondents had received T&I training (p. 201), which led Katan to think that 'the discrepancy between the academics' optimism regarding the relevance of translation studies and its impact on the workplace, and the reality could be simply due to time' (p. 204) and that the recent focus on academic and theoretical content in T&I training – what Katan calls 'academicization', also labelled 'academisation' by Pöchhacker (2004, p. 30) – could soon change that situation. Katan's hypothesis was that younger university-trained professionals would be more exposed to theory and more convinced of its benefits than the majority of older practitioners who were trained in vocational-oriented programmes or who learned the skills on the job and started practising without any knowledge of or interest in theories of T&I, and who do not see any benefit from theory and research in their daily practice. With the available data of his survey, Katan decided to investigate this assumption and compared responses from professionals of different age groups. The finding was that there was no difference between the youngest and the oldest practitioners in terms of the interest and usefulness of theory for the profession, and Katan concluded that 'we can see no perceivable increase in the appreciation of the fruits of academia over time' (Katan 2009a, p. 204). The younger ones, who are more likely to have been trained in university programmes offering some academic content in T&I, seem to lose sight of academia and of the theoretical knowledge they received once they become practitioners, possibly because of the above-mentioned apparent uselessness of research theories in their everyday professional life.

It is also interesting to note that the divide persists, despite the fact that T&I training is mainly delivered in universities along more academic lines promoting theory and research. Pöchhacker notes in the case of interpreting research, for example, that 'Notwithstanding this evolution of interpreting research, in the academic environment a tension between the vocational and academic orientations of T&I schools is often felt by professionals, teaching staff and administrators alike' (2004, p. 31).

Another insightful finding from Katan's study relates to the importance of training and training content. As mentioned previously, the majority of practitioners surveyed were positive about the need to undertake training, whether in an academic context or organised by professional peers. But when questioned about the most important and useful content in a training course, respondents classified practice and technically-based skills, T&I strategies that would help them to be job-ready, and T&I electronic tools as 'most important'. However, at the other end of the spread of their replies, they classified T&I theory and ethics as 'less important' (p. 202), far below all the practice-oriented content. Again, there was a lower regard for this irrespective of age. These attitudinal responses point to a perception that the former is less important than the latter and illustrate the alleged gap between the two.

The gap between academic-oriented and theoretical university training and the real world exists but was rarely mentioned in the survey as constituting a real problem. Most practitioners were satisfied with the training they received in universities and with their current work, even if both areas seemed to function as two separate realms. From the survey, which aimed at defining whether Translation was an 'occupation' or could be considered a 'profession', Katan concluded that it could not at the time be defined as a profession, and that to reach the desired professionalisation a new structure of career path, combined with closer links between the academic and professional worlds, should be envisaged by the various industry stakeholders (p. 206).

The difference of perception of the T&I professional can also be discussed as a manifestation of the divide between theory and practice. In another article, using data from the same survey, Katan puts forward the idea that for the last 30 years, 'since the cultural turn [...] and the rise of the functional school', a 'revolution' has taken place in T&I whereby practitioners have gained a new status and have been 'empowered' (2009b, p. 112). Most scholars in the discipline have defended the idea that professionals are now more visible and participate fully in the acts of communication and (re)creation that translations and interpretations are, and are now acknowledged agents in the translational process. 'Practitioners "cross boundaries" (Bassnett 1997) and are "nomads-by-obligation" (Cronin 2003). [...] They are mediators (Hatim/Mason 1990), "cultural mediators" (Katan 1999, 2004), "cross-cultural specialists" (Snell-Hornby 1992), "information brokers" (Obenaus 1995), "cultural interpreters" (Gonzales/Tolron 2006), [...] and "experts in intercultural communication" (Holz-Mäntäri 1984)' (Katan 2009b, p. 112). Katan quotes others for whom 'a professional is "an agent of social change" (Tymoczko 2003), or an "activist involved in re-narrating the world" (Baker 2006, Scarpa 2008) and translation is seen as "a process of power" (Wolf 1995)' (2009b, p. 113). What Katan tells us about the divide between theory and practice is that such a view of the empowered professional is put forward mainly by academics, is not shared by everyone, and even has detractors. John Milton (2001), for example, suggests that 'Translation Studies as an academic area exists as an almost separate domain from that of professional translation ... and that there is minimal contact between these areas' (cited in Katan 2009b, p. 113). Carol Maier (2007) even suggests that professionals are not ready to face the conflicts and responsibilities that increased visibility could involve. I think the idea that these two T&I worlds exist in parallel without really co-existing is to be seriously considered and addressed with a view to finding ways to bridge the 'yawning gap' described by Chesterman and Wagner.

Chesterman's and Wagner's book (2002) is written in the form of a dialogue email correspondence in which Chesterman, a Translation Studies scholar, and Wagner, a translator and translator manager at the European Commission, discuss the usefulness of translation theory and research in the professional world of translators. In the opening page, Wagner presents her views about this usefulness and asserts that they are shared by many of her professional colleagues, who do not see the point of conducting research – studying and analysing – on their everyday occupation. She quotes a colleague of hers (2002, p. 1) who, after reviewing the Routledge Encyclopaedia of Translation Studies, concluded:

> It is a remarkable storehouse of interesting information. But [...] will it help one to become a better translator? Does it help to give the translation profession a feeling of self-esteem and worth? Hardly. From the point of view of my working life, it is interesting but irrelevant.

Chesterman's response (2002, p. 2) was the following:

> Would you pose the same question of other kinds of theory? Should musicology help musicians or composers to become better musicians or composers? [...] From the point of view of a practicing translator [...] theorists are somehow seen to be 'up there', like teachers, in possession of knowledge to hand down, or at least with the duty of finding out such information; and we translators are 'down here'... just tell us what to do, tell us how to do it better, please. [...] Most modern translation theorists find this view very odd. [...] We theorists should seek to be descriptive, to describe, explain and understand what translators actually do, not stipulate what they ought to do. From this descriptive point of view, it is the translators that are 'up there', performing an incredibly complex activity and the theorists are 'down

here', trying to understand how on earth the translators manage. These theorists see themselves as studying the translators, not instructing them.

Both positions are interesting insofar as they are candid, legitimate and sensible. More importantly, they probably represent what most T&I professionals, translators and interpreters, think of research and what most researchers would reply to such criticism or scepticism. As a practitioner and a researcher trying to establish closer links between the two sides of the fence, I believe theory can help professionals if theory manages to formulate sensible options for courses of action and then make them become available for discussion among practitioners. In a 2009 article, Shlesinger discussed what she labelled 'the divide' between T&I practitioners and researchers and the need to cross that divide. She tried to show that the practitioner's intuitions and experience are the researcher's greatest source and that, reciprocally, the researcher's investigations can be useful to the practitioner. She also rightly pointed out that in the field of T&I, most of the research is led by scholars who are, or used to be, practitioners, and that this characteristic should help to reunite both sides, a necessary move for the academic field to have a chance to grow further and for future professionals to be trained even more adequately. This is supported by the results of a recent survey conducted by Pym and Torres-Simon, which showed that out of 305 translation scholars surveyed, '96 per cent of them have translated or interpreted 'on a regular basis', with translation/interpreting being or having been a main or secondary activity for 43 percent of the scholars' (2014, p. 1).

As noted by Shlesinger (2009), all practitioners who are also researchers often hear other practitioners commenting on their practice, their techniques, or asking questions about some elements of their performances. Very often these comments or questions could constitute interesting topics for research, but Shlesinger (2009, p. 3) adds:

> What puzzles me whenever I listen to these musings, each of which could be formulated as a research hypothesis, is that my colleagues rarely see the point of taking these thoughts further, of subjecting them to methodical exploration. "It's not something that can be researched," one of them told me. "Every interpreter is different so how can you tell?" Or: "It's not something you need to check, and how would you check it anyhow"?

Such reluctance by practitioners to willingly participate in research projects can be pointed out as one potential reason for the gap between research and practice. Conversely, it could also be flagged that researchers could try to help practitioners who are severely limited through available free time to further pursue such questions. When listing the various hurdles to develop further interpreting research or the weaknesses in research methodologies to conduct projects on the profession or on practice, Gile also puts forward this same idea: 'Another environmental issue often mentioned in the literature is the reluctance of interpreters to serve as subjects for investigation, which makes data collection problematic. It is difficult to conduct initial experiments with large enough samples of professionals, not to speak of replications' (2009, p. 142).

Even if one can understand why some practitioners feel some discomfort at being observed or even evaluated, interactions and collaboration between researchers and professionals should be promoted on a more regular basis, with a view to reducing the distance between both groups.

The issue for the majority of practitioners who have never been exposed to theory and research in T&I may be that they consider theorising, analysing and conceptualising as something alien to them, cut off from professional practice, or unattainable – 'up there', as Chesterman puts it, and with very few gains for the profession. Many of them acquired their skills through practice-oriented instruction without any reference to research, and they may be practising very well without (Pöchhacker 2010). They may see theorists as external observers who would try to use their findings to evaluate professionals and instruct them about their practice, basing their studies mainly on academic or didactic criteria, irrelevant to the professional realities and useless in practitioners' daily routine. But one could wonder how professionals who support such views could be convinced of the contrary and change their opinion in order to be more open-minded and receptive to T&I theories and research.

> The resistance to research (frequently to 'theory') tends to be more an affair of back-of-the-room whispers, gossip, or furtive complaints that the complex art of performance necessarily surpasses any schemata of theory. The main charge, one might surmise, is that those who study translation and interpreting have not worked as

professionals. They are thus presumed to have a distanced, unrealistic image of what translators do. (Pym & Torres-Simon 2014, p. 1)

It was in order to test the view that T&I scholars or researchers are cut off from the professional reality that these two authors (on behalf of the European Society for Translation Studies – EST) undertook an online questionnaire that was answered by 305 EST members, and which showed, as already mentioned, that 96% of T&I scholars have practised on a regular basis, which means they have core knowledge of the profession and know what T&I practice is about when they talk about it in their scholarly activities. This figure is corroborated by Kelly (2008) whose report on a survey amongst T&I trainers shows that 80% of respondents have at least one full-time year of professional practice in their academic career. This is certainly information that needs to be circulated widely in the T&I community.

Another possible way to explain the divide is also to state that both sides have different understandings and expectations of theory. Academics often conduct their research as an intellectual challenge with a potential for new discoveries, whereas 'for professionals, this approach is a luxury' (Drugan 2013, p. 39), as they would expect concrete, directly applicable and practical recommendations. For Quah, this gap illustrates a failure on the part of academic theorists, for whom 'solving the problems of professionals is a matter of interest only when the approaches they have suggested are involved' (2006, p. 27). In drawing up models, theorists rarely start from professional concerns but rather devise models from theoretical principles and test cases which are rarely drawn from professional translation but from student assignments.

Because of its importance to all the dimensions of the T&I world mentioned so far (i.e. practice, research, training, employers, certification), the issue of quality in translation seems particularly relevant as a good illustration of the theory-practice divide (Byrne 2007; Chesterman & Wagner 2002; Hönig 1998). Quality in translation is constantly assessed and compared in real life. Commissioners and end-users expect to be able to judge what they are paying for and practitioners therefore have a duty to explain, justify and defend their work in terms of quality. And since the 1990s, as in other industries, the translation profession has witnessed a proliferation of international standards (Drugan 2013, p. 69). In parallel to this development, research on both translations and interpretations has also focused strongly on this issue (e.g. Al-Qinai 2000; Clifford 2005; Corsellis 2008; Grbic 2008; Kalina 2002; Kurz 2001; Mossop 2001; Quah 2006; Zwischenberger 2013; Zwischenberger & Behr 2015). In her discussion of this topic, Drugan points out that translation quality is a significant area of disparity between the ivory tower and the 'wordface'. I too believe that measure of T&I quality is an interesting question on which to reflect when one discusses academic/professional relationships and the theory/practice divide, because it is a central concern both in the industry and in translation theory.

There are significant differences between translation and interpreting as far as Quality Management is concerned. This is why the ideas developed in the following paragraphs apply principally to the translation world. Despite long-standing attempts to define and measure T&I quality, no unique standard approach or model has been agreed on. An intrinsic issue when one raises this question is actually that the different models proposed so far assess different elements in the process or the product of translation (Gile 1993; Gouadec 1989; Larose 1998; Lörscher 1992; Orlando 2011). 'There is a particular mismatch between industry and academics here. Some approaches in the theoretical world tend to focus on quality assessment alone whereas others, particularly in the industry, include other aspects such as quality assurance or quality control' (Drugan 2013, p. 36). Contextual elements are also to be taken into account when trying to define or grade quality in T&I. Clients' satisfaction, for example, is an important factor influencing perceptions of quality for end-users of translation services (Mossop 2001).

Reflecting on the reasons for such a divide, Byrne (2007, p. 2) argues that the gap is easily explained by the fact that translation quality is often regarded 'solely from the point of view of academic studies and translation pedagogy, completely shut off from professional practice'. Theorists tend to view industry approaches in translation quality as lacking intellectual rigour or a sufficient underpinning theoretical basis (Al-Qinai 2000; Drugan 2013). On the other hand, the standard view in the profession is that even though theory may be important, 'what can actually be done in the real world is ultimately what matters. [...] Ultimately, the market decides what is good enough for the market' (Drugan 2013, p.

35). As explained by Drugan, the reality is that the two groups are pursuing different goals and are asking different questions when they consider quality. They also have fundamentally different expectations of theory. Very often, the divide exists because of the perspective each group has of translation, a word which can stand either for the process or the product. As Halliday explains (2001, p. 13), linguists believe that theory relates to 'the study of how things are', a rather descriptive approach focussed on the process of translation, whereas professionals see theory as being about 'how things ought to be', with greater focus on the product, i.e. a more normative or prescriptive approach.

The work on quality in Translation Studies conducted by scholars and translation teachers has largely reflected the scholars' and teachers' own concerns than those of readers or end-users, and has mainly revolved round the actual wording of the translation, while the industry tends to focus more on procedures that would lead to a good product. Theorists cannot agree on a model, or even on common definitions (Pym 2003; Dong & Lan 2010); and adding to the confusion is the fact that there does not seem to be any agreed approach within the industry either. The industry, moreover, tends to ignore academic efforts in this area. As Drugan reports (2013, p. 36): 'During hundreds of interviews and research visits to LSPs for [her] book, not a single academic model was mentioned as a way of assessing translation quality in the real world.'

Despite the prevalence of *quality* as a notion applied to practitioners and agencies' standard of performance, and as a metric that can be applied to translation as a research question, it is surprising to find that the concept of quality as a tangible, attainable and measurable attribute has been put forward by only a small number of researchers. Drugan notes (2013, p. 64) that hitherto few detailed models have been presented in academic research, replicated and tested. She singles out the following: House (2014, actually started in the 1970s and refined since then); Larose (1987); Al-Qinai (2000); Williams (2004). Several other scholars (Reiss 1971, for example) have proposed models too, but 'these other approaches have either not presented detailed models or tested their suggestions, or have been explicitly directed at the training of translators rather than application to "real" translations'. On the whole, one could reproach most models proposed thus far by theorists for the absence of any suggestion concerning their classification according to whether they are theoretical or practical, i.e. applied on a regular basis in the real world. Drugan argues that 'this is because professional approaches are either excluded from translation theory or given no more than a cursory attention' (2013, p. 49). In my view, the case of quality as presented above can be used as a clear illustration of the confusion and lack of communication between the two sides of the gap in many other areas of T&I.

3.2 Origins and development of the vocational/academic dichotomy

The relationship between the world's vocational demand and classical academic traditions has not always been easy. Translator training is typically a vocational activity which is often based in, or contingent on, academic settings. This is a core question in this book, which aims at bridging the gap between practice and theory, as it has an obvious impact on the type of curriculum that a T&I programme may adopt. How should the needs of the learner be defined and addressed in a programme of education? How can this programme relate to both the needs of the learner and those of the end-users or other stakeholders, the industry at large? In this sub-section, I will look at the way the vocational vs. academic dichotomy has developed historically in relation to knowledge and teaching, in order to gain insights to facilitate the training of future *practisearchers*.

Several translator trainer scholars like Kelly or Gouadec are somewhat hostile to the idea of translators being trained in a specific kind of university environment – and even more by academics only (a 'preposterous' idea – Gouadec 2007, p. 355) – based on the notion that higher education cultivates academic rationalism/conservatism and that the teaching methodologies employed are what writers such as Kelly (2005) and Kiraly (2000) characterize as transmissionist. Despite such views, translator education and training will very likely remain in academic environments. Indeed, even if translator training is an activity 'falling firmly within the purview of vocational technical colleges', the 'harmonization of higher education under the Bologna Process will inevitably involve re-conceiving undergraduate and graduate studies in many ways' and will 'challenge directly many of the preconceptions of academic rationalism' (Kearns 2008, p. 186). Many institutions will have to re-evaluate their practices in translator training, especially because vocational institutions (in Europe, Australia and East Asia) have recently been merged into university institutional models, as already discussed. Nevertheless, the vocational/academic dichotomy, the place and relevance of theory in a curriculum aiming to train professionals, has traditionally been a crucial issue when discussing T&I training in universities and will certainly remain an issue in the future.

Kearns (2008) argues that one way to discuss the vocational/academic dichotomy and to explain the fact that academic rationalism has been perpetuated in many institutions is to consider its historical development. 'The roots of academia may be found in the seven liberal arts of the historical trivium and quadrivium of the Middle Ages, within which modern fields of study have their origins' (2008, p. 187). The scheme was broadened by the effect of Renaissance humanism. The nineteenth century emphasised the development of universities as research centres with a mission to contribute to 'the cultivation of the mind'. The twentieth century 'saw both teaching and research emphasized and greater demands were placed on universities by societies eagerly seeking both mass education and innovation' (p. 187). However, the preference of academia for the subjects thought most likely to cultivate the mind dates back to the classical Greek distinction between theoretical knowledge and practical knowledge. Knowledge determined social status in ancient Greece and this vocational/academic dichotomy has persisted in modern times, reflecting the same social divides: 'Theoretical knowledge has become associated with a leisured elite and applied knowledge with those who go to work for a living' (p. 189).

It is on the basis of this historical development, and especially the notion of knowledge acquisition embedded in the *cultivation of the mind* concept, that the criticism that academia is cut off from the real world was able to arise. Much of the discourse on universities in the 20th century has been characterised by 'the notion that academics are resistant to examining the practical implications and applications of the subjects which they theorize' (Kearns 2008, p. 190). This is a criticism often heard in the T&I field (Chesterman & Wagner 2002; Gouadec 2007). However, as noted by Kearns but also by Kelly (2008) or Pöchhacker

(2004), the gap between vocational and academic institutions has recently narrowed significantly with the granting of university status to former vocational institutions and also with the increased expectation on the part of many in society that the education universities offer should directly provide graduates with skills which can be applied immediately in specific work environments (Way 2008). This view is also discussed by Hague in relation to the newly defined liberal education; he points out (2013, p. 21) that 'the new definitions emphasize the need for pragmatic and experiential education along with the 'cultivation of the intellect'. For several reasons, translator education fits this modern approach to liberal education quite well.' In an attempt to offer more practical training opportunities within the industry and to give trainees a relevant real-life experience, but also to define training needs with various industry stakeholders, one could point out that placements and internship programmes are offered in most T&I programmes nowadays.

As explained by Kearns, the 20th century saw many changes: traditionally vocational disciplines like pharmacy and engineering have gained academic status following their inclusion in university curricula. Subject areas such as Media Studies and Film Studies have also gained recognition in academia and in particular in the humanities, and it is today hard to imagine a world devoid of references from media, film and or popular culture. Translation Studies shares many similarities with such fields in terms of its recent arrival on the academic scene and the seminal works of Holmes, Toury and Nida, for example, have helped to establish this newly-trodden path. Its academic status today is largely confirmed by the number of current research initiatives as well as publications and journals in the discipline (Kearns 2008, p. 190). Even its interdisciplinary nature (at the crossroads of linguistics, literary studies, cultural studies, communication studies, medicine, law, history, psychology, etc.), questionable to many in academia, may often have been appreciated and seen as a positive new development in the humanities. However, over the last 40 years it is its vocational dimension that has often been detrimental to the recognition of the field and has kept the academic/vocational dichotomy alive. Indeed, T&I programmes 'are almost always obliged to at least possess, and preferably be centred around, a practical element of training' (Kearns 2008, p. 191). Consequently, as already mentioned in the section above related to translator and interpreter training, many of the vocationally-oriented courses which have operated over the last decades, generally taught by professionals, were against theory (Gile 1995; Kearns 2008). The vocational/academic dichotomy has been fuelled over the years by the fact that 'training programmes focused virtually exclusively on the development of those practical vocational skills which were required for a specific career' (Kearns 2008, p. 192). And in the academic world, such an approach has been perceived as not permitting either intellectual reflection or a role for research and theories.

Educational reforms and structural changes in institutions also prompt us to reassess the alleged gap between the vocational and the academic. Universities are pressed by economic demands to provide courses with a more obviously vocational basis. The high studies fees for a Master's degree in T&I in universities in most predominantly Anglophone countries today oblige students either to work part-time or to obtain a loan and, before embarking on the postgraduate journey, prospective students in any course would naturally expect some assurance of potential employability, or at least ensure that what they will be taught will make them immediately employable. On the other hand, as noted by Kearns, 'new academic demands have been placed on many younger universities which have been "upgraded" from being vocational schools' (2008, p. 195), leading to some academisation of the T&I training.

The concern raised by vocational training in a university environment leads to the not-so-new issue of the role of tertiary education and institutions at a given time. The question whether universities should respond to market expectations in the choice of curricula they offer, or whether universities and academics are, to an extent, removed from the real world, has been endlessly debated (Gambier 2005; Kearns 2008). Professionals often contend that academics who are not practitioners, and are ignorant of market realities, cannot and should not be in charge of training future professionals (Gouadec 2007; Kearns 2008), and that one should be sceptical if those academics who would have the appropriate skills and expertise to train translators become involved in organisations or associations representing practitioners. Should T&I training be done in universities only? Following Pöchhacker's notion of 'meta-level training', I mentioned earlier the fact that training can also be organised by professional associations (FIT, AIIC or national ones), by Institutions (e.g. the DG Translation and DG Interpretation at the European Commission), by large companies or agencies. As Pym argues (2006, p. 50): 'There are many situations in which translators can be effectively trained – on the job, in short courses, by mentoring, etc.' However, the current reality, whether T&I professionals like it or not, is that translation classes are indeed mainly taught by academics at tertiary level: either by language teachers in language programmes as a linguistic activity leading to the acquisition of some linguistic skills, or by T&I academics in translation programmes aiming to train future professionals. Even if this is the reality, they might not be the best equipped to teach the vocational skills needed to be easily employable in the T&I industry.

This question also relates to what is taught in translation classes in university language departments, and to the type of curriculum designed and implemented in universities. Relying on a report released by the European Council of Modern languages (ECML) in 2000, Kearns comments that one main concern in the industry and the profession relates to the distinction which should be made between translation in an educational context and professional translation and the fact that what is taught in the classroom remains artificial compared to the real-life conditions of professional translation (2006, p. 44). In this regard, it is important to note that, in recent years, a new discourse in tertiary educational studies and curricula renewal has developed: it concerns transferable skills, which are seen as preparing the student to be mobile and adaptable between various jobs, whereas traditional vocational skills equip the student for a more specific job. It is often this new set of transferable skills that academics are in charge of in T&I training in the university context, a function which legitimises further the need for their presence in the training process. An emphasis on transferable skills was imposed on academia in the late 1980s in the UK, following the publication of several white papers underlining the lack of certain general vocational skills amongst students, who were therefore not well-equipped for the job market. The idea was that the acquisition of transferable skills would enable professional mobility both within and between sectors and would provide students with 'the generic capabilities which allow people to succeed in a wide range of different tasks and jobs' (Kearns 2008, p. 203).

Another contrast revealed in the ECML report was that between translation taught in the academic environment of a university and in the more vocationally-oriented T&I schools, which would obviously affect T&I training and was also fuelled by what Ekaterina Draganova, one of the ECML rapporteurs, described as: '[T]he arrogant contempt that academics or universities might feel towards a vocationally oriented activity and the professionals skilled in translation and interpreting. Conversely, contempt and snobbery was also felt by professional translators and interpreters who claimed they had had better practical training through the rigour of their strictly vocational schools and added that academics and those responsible for designing university courses had no idea of the realities and requirements on the ground' (cited in Kearns 2006, p. 44). The integration of T&I schools into university structures may to some extent 'alleviate the animosity resulting from this dichotomy', but the report emphasized that it still remained a problem in many areas.

The T&I world is dependent on too many variables to allow anyone to decide on a system or a curriculum that will work and will be sustainable. The educational and occupational profile of students is changing; students are changing; the profession is constantly changing (because of societal and technological factors among other things). The most desirable system would be one that allows an ongoing renewal of design within a stable frame, as proposed by Kearns (2008, p. 210):

> A curricular orientation which fosters in students skills which will benefit them in many professional and non-professional contexts is not incompatible with academic or vocational impulses. Rather we believe that it reveals the distinction between these impulses itself to be unworkable and instead proposes that a synergy between both can be enabled by enlightened educational practice.

It is for these reasons that translators and interpreters continue to be trained in universities. And to those who would question the relevance of that situation, I would reply that our societies look up to the high intellectual standing and value that universities have always represented and continue to represent. And, as I have already mentioned, it is in those institutions as they are today that one might find the right place for the synergies between the academic and the vocational to be capitalised on: researchers could shed new light on practice, practitioners could inform about changes and new realities in the profession, and educators and trainers could adapt the curriculum accordingly. My view is that it is only in such environments that the 21st century *practisearcher* will be able to tick all boxes: engagement in research, practice and teaching.

3.3 How can the divide be crossed?

I will explore here possible ways of crossing the divide between practice and research and will try to identify and suggest strategies to train 21st century translators and interpreters which will better equip them to cope with both practical and academic demands imposed on them by their professional environment.

The first point I would like to make is that if T&I training institutions wish to train and educate future professionals in response to a 21st century context, more linkages and bridges must be established between the T&I industry, T&I research and T&I training institutions. Training should be conducted in an environment where representatives of all areas are involved in class activities. As mentioned earlier, this requires that institutions accept the employment of professionals as well as academics. Employing only professionals would run the risk of offering only a vocational training and little academic knowledge, whereas employing only academics would run the risk of offering only an academic education in T&I and insufficient insights into the profession. In this context, I would advocate the presence and recognition of the status of *practisearchers* in every T&I institution, facilitating a situation in which those who teach also conduct research and are officially given the possibility to continue to practise.

Daniel Gile coined the term *practisearchers* in the early 1990s, in a context where some researchers in interpreting challenged the only existing paradigm at the time, that of the Paris school. Gile defined *practisearchers* as 'practitioners-cum-researchers who wished to adopt a more scientific approach in their investigation of interpretation' (1995b, p. 15), in opposition to those practising interpreters who carried out studies and developed training curricula only from 'personal speculation'. In the literature, the term has since then been widely used to differentiate those practitioners who have an interest in theory and research from practitioners only or from academics only, and both in translation and interpreting (e.g. Pöchhacker 2004; Sawyer 2004; Shlesinger 2009; Snell Hornby 2006). I will use the term in the following pages in this broader sense, but taking into account those T&I practitioners-researchers who are involved in the training and education of translators and interpreters. As Setton notes, 'the most productive way for theory and research to feed back into practice is still through the laboratory of interpreter training' (2010, p. 4). As I see practice, research and training as being interrelated in a cyclical way (i.e. practice can inform research which can inform training which will in its turn inform practice), I would like to argue that to bridge this practice/research gap, we need to train tomorrow's T&I professionals as *practisearchers*.

In my view, enabling many more practitioners to speak out, to become proactive and to find ways to turn their experience into a more academic form of knowledge, and to conceptualise their basic questions, would help to cross the divide. I also believe that training students to conceptualise practical discoveries and to use and observe the benefits of theories in their practice, as well as to realise that some types of research can benefit instructional practices, would also be a good step towards reconciling both sides. Because of these beliefs, I will hereafter try to demonstrate that there is a place for putting research findings and theory into practice, but their application will be possible essentially through training.

3.3.1 Can practice and research inform each other?

One way to change the situation might be to bring into the profession useful practical input produced by research. For example, as Wagner puts it, as a practitioner she would be attracted by the idea of developing 'a toolkit of theoretical concepts that translators should bring to their job' (2002, p. 7); once named, these tools could give translators a common language in which to talk about translation. Otherwise, to her as to many, theory is too abstract. Quoting two of her colleagues, Wagner notes that for professionals 'the crucial part is becoming consciously aware of WHAT you are doing and HOW and deliberately applying that awareness in order to develop even more effective working routines' (2002, p. 68). This is a very good point: theorising can be useful if practitioners become aware of what they are doing when they practise. More awareness can bring self-criticism and opens door for improvement and better practice. Elaborating on the work of Chesterman and Wagner, Drugan suggests that theorists and practitioners have long recognised that researchers should spend more time studying real professionals in real action, and that at a time of drastic changes in the industry, 'this is truer than ever' (2013, p. 192). This clearly poses the question of what sort of research should be carried out to benefit the professional, or for example whether research should be product- or process-oriented. Would a more process-oriented formative approach in studying their daily occupation (generally more focussed on the product) help T&I professionals to feel more confident in their work, or help them to make better strategic choices in their translation or interpretation choices? Shlesinger develops a similar idea when she notes that a focus of theory should be put on what a practitioner may learn from the findings of research and the efforts made in applying these to their actual practice, whether in written translation or in interpreting. But she also asks: 'What kind of research will continue to provide such findings and what kind of interface between researchers and practitioners will improve the chances of learning from them?' (2009, p. 4).

Elaborating on this, Shlesinger (2009) provides interesting statistics on articles published over a 5-year period in *Interpreting, the International Journal of Research and Practice in Interpreting* and on the types of research areas covered in that publication and made available to readers of the journal. The various themes covered can be grouped, the major groups being: modality of interpreting, modes of interpreting, pedagogy, and working conditions (especially remote interpreting). Her point is to indicate that as the majority of these papers covered research on practical aspects of the profession, on skills and competence, they could be of interest to practitioners and even could influence their practice, should they read them. She also draws attention to the fact that a full 50% of the papers surveyed centred on pedagogical issues or made pedagogical suggestions, insisting that 'the divide is being crossed not only between practitioners and researchers but also between practisearchers and teachers, who seek ways of harnessing research to improve their methods of imparting the elusive skill of interpreting' (2009, p. 8). In her attempt to develop further the idea that the gap could be bridged if practitioners were more connected with research and were encouraged to undertake research projects, she reviews ten examples of theses and dissertations, written by post-graduate students or non-tenured academics who are also practitioners, which all provide 'enlightening implications for practitioners'

(2009, p. 12). For Shlesinger, if practitioners found an interest in reading publications in T&I Studies or engaged in research activities, the two sides of the gap could be bridged. This is also what is suggested by Chesterman in relation to translators (2002): the situation could change if practitioners wrote more about translation. In doing so, there might be more empirical studies to determine the conditions in which better practical outcomes are reached, and professional activity might become more grounded in a body of knowledge.

I share the view that one way to cross the divide would be to find ways to engage practitioners in research activities, not as objects or subjects only, but also as authors/leaders. The main issue here is that even if someone managed to convince them that their very practical questions, stemming from their experience, could become interesting subjects of analysis and research, something that can be researched, many would feel extremely insecure and therefore reluctant to embark on any research project. Existing research models, amenable and relevant though they are, may still contain obstacles that hinder the participation of practitioners. To contemplate the idea that they could be interested in research, or even undertake research, most practitioners would need to be trained to undertake research and not simply comment on their practice. The abstraction that goes with most research, and is essential for the theory to fulfil its explanatory task, holds little appeal for those whose daily activity is very concrete and practical. However candid and more grounded researchers are when they say that 'methodical exploration' is rather 'down here' – while professionals are 'up there' – (Chesterman &Wagner 2002, p. 2), many practitioners would initially find the task of conducting research either intimidating or too abstract and disconnected from who they are and what they do. One way of mitigating such a feeling would be, as advocated by Gile *à propos* interpreting in the public sector, to encourage practitioners to consider exploratory research into more practical topics such as working conditions, professional qualifications, and role perceptions. According to Gile (2009a, p. 138), such projects are

> methodologically less sophisticated than experimental research and could encourage more scholars to engage in empirical research. Their studies could provide them with good basic hands-on training which could then lead to more ambitious designs.

Moreover, as most projects on such topics would be directly relevant to the needs of translators, interpreters and their clients, they 'could help bridge some of the perceived gap between research and practice and overcome some of the hostility of practitioners towards the academic world'. This is in my view an area where *practisearchers* could definitely be productive and useful to the whole T&I community.

Another way of making research more appealing to many T&I practitioners might be to attempt to transpose to T&I Studies research models and approaches used in other disciplines to recognise the value of practice in an academic environment. In dealing later with potential future directions, I will discuss the idea that concepts such as *practice-led research, practice-as-research* or *practice-informed research*, used by practitioners-researchers in the visual arts, the performing arts or the creative arts may be beneficial concepts for the T&I community.

I have so far discussed the idea that it may be possible to bring theory and practice in T&I closer and I have tried to identify how the divide between practitioners and researchers could be crossed, based on the belief, which I uphold, that this divide indeed exists. Interestingly, the question has also been dealt with from another angle. Not everyone in the translation and interpreting community is fully convinced of the need to narrow the gap, which has even been referred to as 'an alleged gap' (Wadensjö 2011). In her article (2011, p. 13), Wadensjö discusses

> the development of what can be seen as two competitive trends – an urge for evidenced-based interpreting practice on the one hand and, on the other hand, a interest in studies of interpreting as an academic field in its own right, i.e. studies designed to explore and explain how interpreting happens.

In response to a certain urge for narrowing 'a supposed gap between theory and practice', Wadensjö suggests 'keeping a critical distance'. As a *practisearcher* herself, Wadensjö began conducting research to raise awareness about 'a marginalized but growing phenomenon in society' and 'to make people in and outside the academia realize the complexity of the interpreter's job, as well as to make candidate interpreters realise how they ought to perform their professional role' (2011, p. 15). Undertaking her research, she became aware of the various questions and themes developed in Interpreting Studies to promote and improve interpreting as a profession, but she also questions today the relation of these issues to the advancement of the academic field itself. Indeed, if research is only carried out for the benefit of the profession, what benefit does the discipline itself gain? This leads us again to the question raised above by Chesterman: if theorists 'see themselves as studying the translators [and] not instructing them' (2002, p. 2), then should translation theory even aim to help professionals to become better? Conducting research helps us to explain and understand how some phenomena work or happen and leads to the acquisition of new knowledge. But does this knowledge apply in practice? If research in T&I is to explain how translating and interpreting happen, should it be undertaken to help practitioners? Wadensjö advocates keeping a critical distance between theory and practice, maintaining that some researchers still conduct research to explore and describe, but do so in a prescriptive way, 'an old tradition' to say how practitioners ought to perform, even if there is a 'recent call for evidence-based practice [...] a wish amongst researchers to bridge the gap between theory and practice' (2011, p. 16). This idea actually may reveal not only a gap between practitioners and researchers but also a gap between different types of researchers: the prescriptive researchers and the researchers responding to evidence-based practice. This also raises serious questions about the role of research. Hale and Napier (2013, p. 11) sum up the concepts as being either 'basic or applied research', whereby 'basic research aims to advance knowledge regardless of its application, whereas applied research aims to investigate real-world problems with the aim to solve them'. They remind us, however, that they remain interrelated, as conceptual research and empirical research are.

In most academic disciplines in which training leads to a professional qualification, the role of research could indeed be dual: having relevance for the practice itself but at the same time being conducted to develop and enhance the discipline itself, without necessarily any useful outcome for practice. As Dimitrova argues, 'we must allow for different kinds of research, treating all kinds of questions, such that are relevant to the professional practice and/or to society at large, as being one important type, but also such that are of theoretical interest, without any immediate applications in sight' (cited in Wadensjö 2011, p. 19). As mentioned above, different kinds of research may imply different kinds of researchers who may have different interests in conducting research for a discipline according to certain research models. In the recent EST survey conducted by Pym and Torres-Simon that I mentioned earlier, the surveyed scholars were asked if there *should* be a relation between their scholarly work and their practice. Even though 74% replied that there was a relation in their case, 26% responded that there *should not* be a relation, and overall the idea was that 'the relationship can be beneficial but is not a sine qua non' (Pym & Torres-Simon 2014, p. 12). This needs to be recognised: research does not need to be useful for practice. Gile (2009b, p. 35) even suggests that trying to improve practices through research in T&I Studies may not always be the most relevant way:

> When asking what kind of research needs to be conducted in Translation Studies, one question is *what* interests it is supposed to serve: improvements in Translation (translation and interpreting) quality, in working conditions, in training, in communication between cultures etc.? If so, other types of action, including lobbying and awareness-raising operations conducted by professional bodies could be so much more efficient that the contribution of Translation Studies could be considered negligible or even counter-productive.

Chesterman and Wagner's title asks if theory *can* be useful, not if it *should*. Of interest to this work and to the discussion on bridging the gap between theory and practice is the idea that theory may turn out to be useful even if it has no duty to be. This is where the role of *practisearchers* may become crucial, as they can become the ones who reveal how research can be useful to practice, even when the first intention of a research project does not appear to be practice-oriented. In the same vein, Shlesinger closed her reflections on the subject by putting forward the idea that researchers draw their research material from practitioners' insights; and even though these insights are not enough in themselves, they are an invaluable source, 'a precious backdrop for our reading and researching and querying'(2009, p. 14). Hale and Napier also maintain that 'interpreter intuitions are often instrumental in guiding research agendas' (2013, p. 235). Even if he supports the idea that research can also be done less subjectively by non-professionals, Gile too advocates the participation and input of practitioners in T&I research projects 'in order to avoid the blatant mistakes of early investigators which were invoked by Seleskovitch to justify research on interpreting by professional interpreters' (2009a, p. 138).

In their recent EST survey, Pym and Torres-Simon surveyed 252 T&I scholars who are still engaged in a professional T&I activity, are research-active and are involved in T&I teaching (i.e. are *practisearchers*). Questions were asked about their views on the relation between their professional practice and their research activities. 75% saw a major relation between the two activities which 'can nurture each other', but some of them expressed also the need to try to keep them separate and therefore get a feeling 'of doing something else' (2014, p. 9).

For many, professional practice informs their scholarly work, provides them with an adequate framework for analysis, and improves their understanding of theoretical data. Some also maintained that practice motivates research and provides topics and data for research, as well as case studies. Several respondents explained that their own research stemmed from questions generated by their practice, and others use their translation or interpreting work as useful data for the studies they carry out. For others, T&I practice helps with networking and in particular with finding participants for research projects. There were also indications that professional practice gives credibility to researchers, especially when the research is carried out with industry stakeholders. The relation was not seen as unilateral only and some respondents explained that while practice informs scholarly work, scholarly work also informs practice, and the relation between both can be seen as a two-way street with no gap whatsoever between the activities. Several respondents recognised that their practice benefits from some theories and that theory could be sterile if it does not support practical examples. For others theory helps professionals in their decision-making process as it allows them to better analyse the task of translating or interpreting. Scholarly work informs practice in the sense that, for some, professionals cannot seriously pursue their activity without reflecting on the processes or the framing ideologies involved. Finally, practice and scholarly work were seen as connected through teaching, as the knowledge that some teachers gain from their practice can be passed on to students before they themselves experience the same situations. Some indicated that this practical knowledge also helps the teachers/researchers, since it makes them more secure about their teaching and research activities. On the negative side of the practice/research relation, however, some respondents indicated that even if they would like to be more involved in T&I professional activity, working in a scholarly and academic environment somehow impedes engagement with practice because of lack of recognition of this practice as scholarly work, because of lack of time or even because of legal prohibition.

These valuable responses from *practisearchers* indicate that there are plenty of benefits in seeing T&I staff in higher education involved in all facets of the discipline, but also a few impediments to strengthening the relation between these facets. There may still be a long way to go before we see well-accepted and well-integrated *practisearchers* fully recognised in T&I training and education in academic environments, but, as indicated above, there are reasons to be optimistic. In the meantime, it is important to value each side of the divide for its own right and importance and also to accept, as Shlesinger remarks, that 'in any case, theory feeds into practice and practice feeds into theory, as our discipline and its sub-disciplines diverge and converge and enter into symbiotic relations with other disciplines as well. […] It is, in the end, an evolutionary process' (2009, p. 14).

Based on the assumption that, to bridge the gap, we need to train future professionals as *practisearchers*, and to recognise that T&I training institutions should employ such profiles in their programmes, I would like now to discuss how to define and implement such training and what place research and theory should occupy in training.

3.3.2 The role of research and theory in T&I training

Having explored how the involvement of current practitioners in research projects conducted in T&I institutions could benefit both sides of the divide and help bridging the gap, I now would like to discuss the way training has lately become more and more academised, and also to reflect on the presence of theory and research in the training and education of future T&I professionals. One aspect not to be ignored in this discussion is that training may be the only way for research findings and theory to be considered in practice. As underlined by Gile (2013, p. 2) in relation to the increasing amount of T&I research material made widely available through journals and publications,

> Of what use is it if colleagues who might gain from reading it do not take the trouble to do so? The gap, indifference and sometimes outright hostility of many practising translators and interpreters towards theory and research in general is well known to

all. But one might expect a somewhat more open attitude from instructors in academic training programs.

This would imply of course that those in charge of T&I curriculum design, training and education work at integrating this new knowledge in their pedagogy and courses, which so far has been 'disappointingly slow' (Setton 2010, p. 6).

3.3.2.1 Academisation of T&I training

As I mentioned earlier, an increasing number of trainers have taken an interest in research since the 1980s, and research in T&I has developed quickly according to various changing paradigms. Initially focused on professional skills and competence taught in schools and institutes, training has shifted towards a more scientific, theory-driven approach under the impulse of several scholars whose training models developed from a cognitive, process-oriented paradigm. Moreover, as discussed in the previous sub-section, several educational and institutional reforms in higher education have forced schools to be merged into larger academic environments in which the combination of teaching and research is a fundamental principle (Kearns 2008; Pöchhacker 2010). It is in this new context that T&I programmes integrated into university research-oriented departmental structures have seen more and more of their staff conduct research, their students increasingly exposed to theoretical analysis and reflection, and many doctoral works completed.

The challenge of T&I programmes today, however, would be to show that the two components – research and teaching – can, and perhaps should, be more closely related. As Pöchhacker has written (2004, p. 32): 'the academisation of [interpreter] training is the critical link between professionalization and the emergence of autonomous research'. This is a key point when considering how to train future T&I professionals to become more familiar with research methodologies and to conduct their own practice-oriented research projects with a view to bridging the gap between practice and theory. Training could be the pivotal element in the vocational/academic equation if those who teach in T&I institutions are well aware of the realities of both worlds. Pym argues that 'tension in industry-academy relation can have benefits too: it allows trainers to act as critical friends, scrutinising industry assumptions and offering insights from theory' (2006, n. p.).

Discussing the evolution of research in Interpreting Studies, Setton also states (2010, p. 3) that:

> Today, Interpreting Studies owes its existence to the commitment of a few enthusiastic researchers and the thesis requirements of a few schools rather than to any direct appeal from the profession or recognised application of its findings to the practice of interpreting. It can thus only survive as part of a self-nourishing cycle in which the pivotal link is interpreter training.

Such views promote the idea that the issue is not only about practice and theory but also concerns research about training, for training, and in training environments, as well as the question of who should carry out such research activities.

Because of a lack of evidence-based research with a focus on professional and practical issues, not enough of the research done in T&I is relevant for teaching and learning. Several scholars (namely, Gile, Pöchhacker and Setton) argue that to create more pathways between practice and research, research into training and education is needed. To create a friendlier research-oriented training environment, Pöchhacker (2010, p. 3) advocates the idea of conducting research useful for teaching and learning and aimed at findings that would be helpful for the trainees in the classroom (e.g. studies on markets, skills, etc.) or would allow them to answer questions related (for example) to the cognitive complexities of the interpreting task. According to him, data from authentic professional events are still lacking 'for issues which would require an evidence-based basis for strategic guidance in the classroom' (2010, p. 4). He also claims that despite the number of university-level T&I training programmes worldwide very little is known about what actually happens in the classroom and not enough research on instructional practices has been carried out. These comments echo those made by Gile more than twenty years ago (1990, p. 33) about the poor impact of training-oriented research:

> It does not seem to have had any significant effect on training methods and results except in courses given by the researchers themselves, and sometimes in the schools where they teach, but on the whole, interpretation instructors prefer to keep their personal, most often traditional methods, and take no heed of research.

It is not clear that things have changed much twenty years later, but the academisation of T&I training, as well as the greater availability of research findings in academic journals, should be a source of optimism, since those who will join the ranks of teaching staff in the future will have been more exposed to theory and research in their own studies or professional development. Also, as Hale and Napier indicate in relation to interpreting research (2013, p. 180), 'the possibilities for interpreter education research are huge' and 'interpreter educators are becoming more mindful of the role of Interpreting research and the need to link research to education and practice, both in terms of doing research on interpreting for interpreter educators, and also doing research on interpreter education'.

As alluded to earlier, one way to disseminate and promote the findings of research on education, and to better map and maybe standardise what is happening in T&I classrooms worldwide, would be to have more and more accessible journal articles and to publish books or textbooks on the didactics of T&I. This could be done with a view to invite practitioners who have a teaching activity but did not receive an academic T&I training to gain a better pedagogical and theoretical understanding and grasp of what they do or could do when teaching. A recently published volume edited by Dörte Andres and Martina Behr, from the University of Mainz in Germersheim, fulfils exactly such an ambition (Andres & Behr, 2015). Andrew Gillies' practice book for conference interpreting students or trainers (2013) and James Nolan's textbook on interpretation techniques and exercises (2012) are two other good examples worth mentioning.

Discussing the role of research in training, Gile (2009b, p. 37) points out that research is frequently undertaken by students for their MA theses or other types of research projects required in their degrees, and that they therefore enhance their research skills, acquiring 'a good sense of what research entails and hopefully rigorous working methods. This is a good basis for the acquisition of more advanced techniques later.' Indeed, once empowered in the research process, graduates of T&I programmes could choose to pursue their studies by undertaking doctoral research or to work as practitioners only, but as practitioners capable of carrying out experiential research if they should wish to do so later on. Echoing Pöchhacker, Gile suggests that through research into training, 'it might be a good idea to guide students and young researchers towards empirical studies which would contribute both to our factual knowledge of the world of Translation and to enhancement of their research competence' (2009b, p. 38).

As mentioned above, the lack of research findings on professional and educational practices providing reliable factual knowledge reduces the opportunities for educators in T&I to apply new teaching methods in their classroom activities and to improve training practices. Therefore, it is crucial to find ways to develop more research activities in this area (Mikkelson 2013). This poses the question of who should carry out necessary research activities on teaching and learning as well as how to carry out such research. I would suggest that training and education in T&I nowadays should focus on skills and competence, but also on empowering students or practitioners in the research process and in research methodologies. In relation to research on interpreting, Pöchhacker (2010, p. 7) writes:

> more and more scholars with a background in interpreting have sought to acquire the research skills needed to conduct state-of-the-art projects in a given domain. Most typically, new research findings in interpreting studies come from doctoral researchers who are graduates of an interpreter training program and, more often than not, teachers of interpreting.

If that is the case, I believe that practitioners-researchers-teachers with this profile should become tomorrow's *practisearchers* and conduct the exploratory research lacking in the discipline. They could be students undertaking a doctoral project after having been taught the necessary methodology for such research on top of the vocational T&I skills dispensed in the programme, or experienced professionals who were trained and given access to the methodology needed to carry out their research project.

3.3.2.2 Vocational training or academic education?

As Kearns stresses (2008, p. 194), from the perspective of translator training, there are certain educational arguments that minimise the existence of a theory/practice gap. Pym's minimalist notion of translator competence (as already discussed), for example, supports the idea that there is an indivisibility of theoretical and practical knowledge which must be recognised when considering translation competence, and that some theoretical training is desirable in translator education. Representing several prominent T&I training institutions worldwide, CIUTI similarly stresses the dual identity of T&I education as being both oriented towards professional practice and guided by academic research. Training is indeed in my view the most productive conduit between theory and practice. It is through a multifaceted approach to teaching that T&I training institutions will manage to take up the challenges posed by the rapid changes which are constantly transforming the industry. It is through a curriculum which includes translation and interpreting exercises, research projects, theoretical seminars, practical and technical workshops, internships, student placements, industry representatives' presentations and *practicum* hours within the industry that trainees will gain knowledge, competence and skills required in the 21st century T&I world. As Gile (1995, 2005) frequently notes, it is thanks to both theoretical knowledge and a reflective practice focussing at some stage of the training on the process of translation or interpretation that awareness will be raised amongst students and professionals that translating is not an automatic act, but a decision-making act of communication which requires critical thinking and for which applied theoretical knowledge can be as useful as practical skills. In this regard, it may be relevant to consider research and teaching informed by practice as a way of balancing vocational training and academic education. Creating room for practice but also for representations of the industry in an academic curriculum should not be seen as threatening academic freedom and independence.

    I would recommend that a T&I course be designed on the basis of an accurate picture of the environment in which graduates will exit the course. Whether they pursue their studies or join the profession, the course designers must know what will be required of graduates in their future environment (whether it is academia or a given industry market). As advocated by Neff (2015), provisions should also be made in T&I curricula to develop didactic approaches to deal with professionalisation so that students are well-informed about the market they are about to operate in. This demands sound knowledge and up-to-date information about these contexts. Then the activities dispensed in the course should be decided on the basis of this description on the one hand, and on the profiles of typical beginners admitted to the course on the other. All activities and exercises should be structured according to a progression that should be clear to both students and teachers and should include practical and theoretical elements adapted to T&I skills and competence.

'We do not teach translation, we train translators': these are the words with which Gambier called for translator training to be relevant to the demands of industry, so that graduates of T&I can be job-ready when they complete their T&I degree (interview with Neves 2005). His view is shared by others (Gouadec 2007), who have pleaded for a move away from lecturer-centred methodology in T&I training. Kearns, on the contrary, argues – even though he views positively the idea that graduates should be aware of and ready for their future industry – that as T&I educators 'we do not train translators, we teach translation: we train, teach and otherwise attempt to facilitate the education of *students* of translation' (2008, p. 207). This difference of perspectives also reveals the existence of a divide in training as well (Way 2008) and poses the question of the degree of specialisation for trainees: should we train students and develop their *translator competence* so that they can respond to industry demands, or should we ignore such market directions and provide students with an academic knowledge and legacy – a *translation competence* – which will allow them to adapt and transfer skills for a potentially wide range of jobs in the industry? As Calvo notes (2011, p. 13):

> There has been considerable debate on whether translation programmes should be exclusively market-oriented or rather based on classical rationalism (theoretical knowledge; e.g., philology-based approaches) or both. Curricula composed according to this polarisation either contemplate: vocational schemes which tend to respond to descriptions of what translators should know or be able to do in order to be competent professionals in a specific industry (translator skills or competence); or academic approaches which rather focus on descriptive, more theoretical translational conceptions of language, intercultural transfer, (literary) translation analysis, linguistics, etc. [...] While most vocational proposals choose highly professionalised and specialised competence models, other curriculum schemes defend a more transferable translation competence approach in line with contemporary employability-led policies.

The concept of transferable skills, discussed previously, has been embraced by many universities which do realise the need to equip graduates with skills and competence that may be applied in a variety of jobs (Way 2008). This being said, in the case of T&I, curriculum designers would agree nowadays that the course must be dispensed on the basis of a balance between training in vocational skills and education in the theories of the discipline. The task of T&I trainers is therefore a dual one in so far as they have to enable their trainees 'to acquire both the generic and the specific competences required for professional translation', but must also provide their graduates with 'the tools to ensure that they are capable of maintaining and upgrading their competences throughout their professional working lives' (Way 2008, p. 89).

Gouadec (2007), for example, is among those who advocate that trainers should not design training for a narrowly defined market but rather to empower trainees to be able to apply for a large variety of positions in the industry and to be competitive freelancers. T&I training should combine methodology and theory on the one hand, and practical experience on the other, in a teaching/learning process based on hands-on experience and guidance. 'The learning process must be related to know-how and be similar to that of skilled craftsmen, who first learn their craft by watching and working alongside others and then by being closely tutored as they move on to practice' (Gouadec 2007, p. 332). It is also important to define clearly the learning outcomes of a course and to assess students at the end of their course on the same basis as when they apply for a job in the T&I industry. Professionally-based quality standards must therefore be defined and applied when assessing translations and interpretations, for example, and especially when awarding qualifications. At the same time, and given that the T&I professional environment has changed a great deal in the last decades and is in perpetual movement, it is also true that training courses must evolve as a consequence. Curricula have to be renewed, they cannot stay the same. Students must, for example, be exposed to new technologies or new contexts and teachers must bring those developments into the classroom. As technologies have a major impact on professional practices and strategies, this raises questions about how technological issues are addressed in a training context. It is for all these reasons that future graduates need to be exposed to some of the theories underlying current developments in T&I Studies and be introduced to research principles so that they can reflect on their practice and on the processes at stake and not simply become 'mere 'operatives' in an increasingly automated translation process' (Gouadec 2007, p. 336). Discussing the place of theory in interpreting training and its impact on interpreting practice, Setton argues that only the successful training of excellent interpreters will make a difference in the future. Today's training implies that course designers and instructors are capable of taking 'the measure of what is universal vs. what is individually variable, applying the findings of cognitive science and pedagogical theory respectively, so that theory is converted into practice through the learning process – theory implemented through people in their diversity' (Setton 2010, p. 5). Theory should indeed be present in the T&I classroom but be introduced in a relevant and sensible way at various training stages, and the 'literature should only be drawn upon if a clear, lively and pedagogical picture can be extracted that trainees can immediately connect with their own experience' (Setton 2010, p. 13).

A constant criticism directed at T&I courses dispensed in an academic environment is that theory occupies too much space in the curriculum, at the expense of practice (see, for example, Chesterman & Wagner 2002 for an extended debate on this topic). For some (Kearns 2006; Pym 2005), the answer to such criticism may be to support traditional academic structures as well as the theorising which gives academics some institutional and intellectual power as it may not necessarily be a bad thing. As Pym notes, 'with it, changes in the profession can eventually lead to changes in institutional training programmes. Without it, we would be back to medieval apprenticeships' (2005, p. 6). The argument that excessive attention to theory deprives trainees of practical experience misses the main point: 'It is the theories themselves which need to be improved by being informed by professional knowledge so that they may be of better service to both trainers (even if this does mean challenging the institutional practices in which they work) and professionals' (Kearns 2006, p.54). Gouadec supports this view when he notes (2007, p. 356):

> Theory and research must underlie every aspect of the translator training course, but in such a way that they help to enhance its professional relevance. This requires extensive research on the part of the faculty members involved so as to provide the solid theoretical grounding on which the course will be based. It is becoming quite clear that this kind of professionally oriented research has already started feeding new translation theories.

Once again, this is where *practisearchers* can play an important role.

This leads me to discuss the types of theoretical content that should be taught to T&I students. In my view, the teaching of T&I theory should be applied theory aimed at making students aware that they will find answers to their practical and professional questions in theoretical models and in certain research findings. As Setton writes (2010, p. 13):

> Training can benefit from 'theory' in at least two dimensions: in understanding the *problem*– the target tasks, intermediate objectives and their attendant cognitive challenges – and to develop effective *solutions* – in other words, pedagogical strategies for reaching them.

Training should prepare students for the profession by equipping them with the appropriate T&I skills and making them as adaptable as possible to the many contexts of work into which they may be plunged, but also to be able to reflect on practice and quickly find solutions to problems thanks to theoretical knowledge. One way of attaining such goals is to clearly differentiate stages in the course where the focus of the activities is either on the process or on the product of translation or interpretation and where different pedagogical tools facilitating the evaluation of such activities are developed and implemented (Gile 1993; Holmes 1972/2000; Pöchhacker 2004). Focussing on the process allows better explications and understanding of difficulties and therefore should allow better remediation exercises too, leading to a better acquisition of practical skills and competence. Gile (2007), for example, suggests developing modules based on theory and methodology focusing on the process, in order to better justify the advice given and the remediation suggested. Such modules are useful for graduates to refer to when they are no longer students and need theory to solve a practical professional issue. Moreover, when translation is viewed as a process of producing and selecting between hypotheses, the importance of theory becomes clear. As Pym notes, theories may help translators to produce more possible versions than they would otherwise have thought of and may help eliminate possible alternatives – it is thus an exceptionally *procedural* (or 'non-declarative') type of theorising that is envisaged (cited in Kearns 2006, p. 55). If theory becomes part of some sort of procedure in the translation process, then it may be considered as no longer separate from competence. As discussed by Kearns, viewing theory in this way can further suit the institutionalisation of translation programmes, in that theory *must* be integrated into classes, rather than being dealt with in lectures. This argument is pertinent to the following section, in which I will discuss the idea that to train tomorrow's *practisearchers*, to bridge the gap between practice and research through the role of training, student-centred/learner-centred/constructivist approaches of teaching and learning should be considered when designing or renewing a T&I curriculum.

3.3.3 A student-centred approach to T&I training and education

I will discuss now how a student-centred/learner-centred/constructivist approach to teaching/learning in T&I could be developed with a view to empowering and emancipating trainees. If trainees are taught how to learn, how to reflect on their learning progress, this might facilitate a self-reflective approach to their practice in the future and a capacity to merge theory and practice more naturally.

As I mentioned in the introduction, I have been teaching for nearly 20 years in different contexts and countries. A constant principle in my vision of the act of teaching is that the role of the instructor is to disappear gradually throughout the learning process. I believe that students will emancipate themselves more easily if the teaching and learning activities are aimed at empowering them. To do so, I think that any curriculum (and T&I education is no exception) should to a certain extent follow a constructivist approach and be centred mainly on the learner/student and take into account problem-solving strategies and metacognitive approaches whereby trainees are given the right academic tools to learn how to reflect on their own practice and learning, or *learn how to learn*. And ultimately, learn how to practice.

As pointed out by Kearns (2006), the teaching environment of the university in Europe and America (and I would add Australia) has recently been moving away from the transmissionist teacher-centred teaching and learning methodologies, which are being challenged by various education scholars who see learning innovation – and the necessity of pedagogical training for university staff – as being essential to the success of mass tertiary education. In the case of T&I training and education, whereby the trainee is supposed to develop both academic and vocational skills and become a job-ready practitioner on graduation day, one may indeed easily understand why training and education dispensed to students in a traditional academic way, in a more teacher-centred transmissionist manner, would run the risk of not fulfilling the empowering role it is supposed to fulfil. To respond to societal and educational changes, curricula in higher education have to be adaptive and regularly renewed to better serve the development of the above-mentioned transferable skills and, as pointed out by Calvo (2011, p. 11)

> teachers are expected to have sound training in teaching and learning strategies and to demonstrate interest in improving their practices, while students are expected to play an active role in the learning process. Curriculum practice and implementation does not focus directly on covering the syllabus or course content, but rather on achieving actual, durable, transferable and significant learning on the students' part.

However, because of the dual vocational/academic nature of the training to be dispensed to future T&I professionals, I would be prudent not to reject fully the teacher-centred, also called 'instructivist' (Westwood 2008), teaching approach which may be appropriate at some stage in the training. Westwood (2008, p. 1) defines contructivists and instructivists as follows:

> Constructivists believe that traditional didactic teaching represents a largely unsuccessful attempt to transmit knowledge in a pre-digested form to learners. They believe that learners must construct knowledge from their own activities. In contrast to the constructivists' view of learning, instructivists believe that direct teaching can be extremely effective.

Even if my teaching practice and my beliefs as a teacher are more constructivist-oriented, I still believe that some T&I teaching activities may be more efficient and more useful if taught in an instructivist manner. Before detailing this question further in relation to T&I teaching practices, I would like to define better what both approaches cover.

3.3.3.1 The constructivist approach vs. the instructivist approach

As defined by Westwood (2008, pp. 2–4), constructivists believe that the very nature of human learning requires that individuals will create their understanding of the world and their knowledge from first-hand experience, action and reflection, and not from having 'pre-digested information and skills presented by a teacher and a textbook'. Constructivists develop their beliefs from the works of early educationalists and theorists like Dewey or Piaget, who also recognised that learning is constructed in an individual manner and can only occur to the extent that new information links successfully with a learner's prior knowledge and experience. Most individuals would indeed acquire knowledge in their everyday life from personal discovery and experience, not from instruction. This view favours teaching methods that focus on the active role played by learners in the acquisition of information, knowledge, concepts and skills (active learning). The idea is that learning must involve students in acquiring knowledge and making meaning for themselves out of interacting with their social and physical environment. In the constructivist classroom, 'the role of the teacher becomes one of facilitator and supporter, rather than instructor' (p. 5). To facilitate interaction in the classroom, group activities, discussions and cooperative learning is highly encouraged. Also, as learners are supposed to acquire targeted skills (be it reading, writing, problem-solving, etc.) by engaging in and communicating about meaningful interactive activities, direct teaching of those skills as well as drills and practice are dismissed.

On the other hand, instructivists believe in the value and efficacy of direct teaching, particularly to attain specific goals in a structured course in which important information and skills are taught in an orderly and sequential manner, and practised, assessed and reviewed regularly. The instructivist approach, also called direct teaching, active teaching or direct instruction, is based on 'the setting of clear objectives for learning, systematic instruction that progresses from simple to more complex concepts and skills, ongoing monitoring of students' progress, frequent questioning and answering, reteaching of content when necessary, practice, application and assessment' (Westwood 2008, p. 9). The underpinning rationale for the instructivist approach is that learning can be optimised if teachers' presentations are so clear that they eliminate all potential misunderstandings and misinterpretations and facilitate generalisation and acquisition. Such explicit instruction aims at presenting information to learners in a form that they can easily access, understand and master.

One of the questions to be posed, in my view, is whether the two approaches are by definition incompatible. My view of the teaching act tends to be more constructivist insofar as I believe in the gradual disappearance of the teacher and in the idea that any curriculum should be designed to progress towards the empowerment or emancipation of the student. However, I also believe that teacher-centred sessions are also useful at different stages of training. Indeed, at different stages of the learning process, presentations of new information by a teacher may facilitate the acquisition and assimilation of knowledge, concepts or notions. Where constructivists would recommend letting students discover this information through interaction and active learning, Yates & Yates, discussing the importance of the role of the teacher as instructor, comment that learning also involves 'exposure to a human being who organises and presents new knowledge to be assimilated and hence reconstructed in the mind of the student' (1990, p. 253). Indeed, even if the idea of involving students in a more active way in the learning process is laudable, one could wonder whether the constructivist approach is relevant to all areas of a curriculum, and appropriate for all students in the classroom. As far as students are concerned, it has been argued in various studies (e.g. De Lemos 2004; Ellis 2005) that students have different learning curves and that for many of them less structured discovery-type activities where learners must acquire or construct essential information can be inefficient for achieving the desired learning outcome. There is evidence too that many students make better progress when they are taught explicitly and directly. As noted by Westwood (2008, p. 6), 'rather than being generally applicable to all types and levels of learning, it is conceivable that constructivist strategies are actually important at a particular stage of learning'. Westwood proposes a model of knowledge acquisition (Jonassen's model of 1992) whereby initial knowledge may well be best served by direct teaching and that advanced knowledge acquisition leading to expertise may benefit most from a constructivist approach.

It is not my intention to list here all the positives and negatives for any of the approaches or to compare them citing various studies, but I would like to signal that, to me, the teaching act is not an act bound to a specific approach and followed in a dogmatic way, but is rather a constant process of adaptation and balance between numerous and changing variables (students, stage of the curriculum, learning objectives, instructors, etc.) and pedagogical lines defined in a specific curriculum. In the case of T&I training and education, and keeping in mind the idea that a well-adjusted mix of theory and practice should be introduced into the curriculum – with a view to training future *practisearchers* –I would argue that some learning objectives would be better attained at some stage of the training if classes were taught in a teacher-centred manner. It is pertinent to point out that minimal guidance from trainers and academics would not necessarily be perceived as acceptable and positive by students who would realise that their needs and expectations when enrolling in a course are not being met. In particular, I think that for activities where the practitioner's authority is crucial (aptitude test, product evaluation against profession-based standards, preparation for final practical examination, etc.), a transmissionist approach may still be the most relevant one. T&I trainees need to learn from practitioners who bring their practical knowledge and experience into the classroom and pass it on to students through active teaching strategies. However, as I mentioned above, the overall progression should aim at empowering trainees through more student-centred activities. This would imply a course designed according to problem-solving and metacognitive activities enabling trainees to reflect on their practice and their learning process.

3.3.3.2 Metacognition and T&I training and education

As noted by Kelly (2008, p. 112), the issue of teaching and of supporting student learning and empowerment in T&I has been dealt with in depth by various trainers such as Kiraly (2000), Gonzalez-Davies (2004) and also Robinson (1997/2003), who have indicated that the emancipation of trainees depends on their capacity to reflect on their progress and their practice and to become actors in the learning process. To gain this aptitude, to learn how to learn, and ultimately to learn how to practice, I believe metacognitive and self-regulation strategies should be introduced into any T&I course. The rationale to link metacognition, the training of *practisearchers*, and the possibility of bridging the gap between practice and research, lies in the idea that trainees will better understand and conceptualise the practice of T&I if they understand the learning and acquisition process of T&I competence and skills, and how theory participates in the acquisition of such competence and skills, before they start working as practitioners. If, throughout their training and education, T&I students are able to identify and understand their personal difficulties in a formative way (Gile 1993; Kiraly 2000), if they are given both practical and theoretical tools to self-assess their work or peer-assess their colleagues' work, if they manage to monitor their performances and reflect on their progress (Choi 2006; Orlando 2011), then I believe that they will be much better equipped to start their career as mature practitioners and researchers. In my view, it is this profound knowledge of the T&I learning process that will enable them to become the future T&I trainers and educators the discipline needs.

Metacognition was originally referred to as knowledge about and regulation of one's cognitive activities in learning processes (Flavell 1979, p. 1). Metacognition is the awareness of the learning process by the learner and the ability to adapt to challenges that occur during this process through effective strategies. Activities such as planning how to approach a given learning task, monitoring comprehension, and evaluating progress toward the completion of a task are metacognitive in nature (Veenman 2006; Wenden 1999). Since metacognition plays a critical role in successful learning, it is important to study metacognitive activity and development to determine how students can be taught to better apply their cognitive resources through metacognitive control. If metacognition is conceived as knowledge of a set of self-instructions for regulating task performance, then cognition is the vehicle of those self-instructions. These cognitive activities in turn are subject to metacognition – for instance, to ongoing monitoring and evaluation processes. Including metacognitive activities in a curriculum gives students the opportunity to monitor their learning and manage their progress (Graham 2007). Research findings show that students with poor monitoring skills do not manage their learning well and perform worse than good monitors. Rivers, for example, shows that students with good skills in self-assessment and self-management are more autonomous students and perform better (2001, p. 280). Autonomous learners are more capable of fixing objectives, defining the content and programme of learning, monitoring and evaluating their progress towards the objectives, their behaviour, their environment, etc., and the findings of Rivers' experiments done in self-directed/self-managed learning show greater productivity and less frustration in students.

Metacognitive knowledge and metacognitive skills should be recognised as complementary components of the broader notion of metacognition (Veenman 2006). Metacognitive knowledge refers to the information learners acquire about their learning, while metacognitive skills, i.e. strategies for planning, monitoring and evaluating, are general skills through which learners manage, direct, regulate and guide their learning. The interest for students in developing their metacognitive knowledge and skills is for them to better understand their personal difficulties for specific tasks (metacognitive knowledge) and to adopt a strategy (metacognitive skills) to monitor and improve their performance. For example, a student may use metacognitive knowledge and skills in planning how to approach a consecutive interpretation exercise in the following manner: 'I know that I (an individual person) have difficulty with note-taking (a specific task), so I will focus first on the macro-structure of the source speech and will work on how to better reproduce it through my notes later on (the chosen strategy).'

Feedback is central to any metacognitive approach. As Veenman (2006) explains, any process of skills acquisition takes time and effort, and teaching and learning activities should be organised around metacognitive skills (as opposed to metacognitive knowledge) which 'have a feedback mechanism built-in' (2006, p. 5). Collective and individual assessment and feedback activities should therefore be planned in any curriculum. Behr (2015) clearly explains the role of feedback and the key to efficient feedback in the classroom: The tasks assigned to students must be clear and concrete, the targets and goals must have been broken down and explained (p. 211), and then feedback on the performance must be given in an objective, benevolent, appropriate, clear and constructive way (p. 212–214), ensuring students understand and are included in the analysis of the performance and the remediation proposed.

Today, collaborative approaches and technologies facilitate the possibility of working with recorded material and enabling teachers and students to exchange their materials effectively (Orlando 2010b). In T&I training, traditional approaches to assessment and self-assessment relying mainly on the teacher as a higher authority are revisited by less conformist tendencies which advocate more active participation of students who should be expected to make a judgement themselves, obviously being provided with metacognitive tools or guides (Arumí & Esteve 2006). Arumí and Esteve have studied the relationship between consciousness of learning and learner autonomy in consecutive interpreting based on the study of self-regulation processes and actions aimed explicitly at encouraging the process of reflection on learning itself. Their conclusion is that drawing up learning-to-learn tools proved a valid way for verbalising metacognitive reflection which should prove useful for teaching purposes. I will present in the 'case studies' part of the book how the use of digital pen technology in the consecutive interpreting classroom allowed the implementation of very positive self- and peer-evaluation activities and feedback, especially in note-taking, as well as the design of remediation strategies judged as very helpful by the students and the teachers of different training institutions.

I too suggest that metacognitive and self-regulation approaches be considered in T&I curricula, as such a focus on students' learning and progress should give them the necessary – indeed indispensable – knowledge of the T&I learning process. This should be more than helpful during their own training, but would also be invaluable knowledge when they pursue their careers as practitioners, researchers or, even more importantly, as T&I teachers. Activities and evaluations differentiating performances as process or as product and incorporating theoretical knowledge applied to practical and professional tasks should be designed and implemented throughout the training period. One important aspect of this teaching philosophy in T&I is to consider evaluations and assessment of performances in various ways. It is essential and beneficial to evaluate trainees against normative profession-based standards at certain stages of their training, but in a training programme with a formative approach, it is also fundamentally important to evaluate them in terms of the process of their knowledge acquisition (Choi 2006; Gile 1993). Different assessment approaches could therefore be defined for different stages and objectives of the course. The following three different types of evaluation could be introduced in the course: *formative* evaluation, based on assessments following the different training stages (this is transparent and serves as a regulation tool); *summative* evaluation, which allows measurement of the sum of acquired competence and knowledge at the end of a specific period; and *normative* evaluation, which is based on defined norms (T&I norms in this case) and aims at assessing an individual against these external norms (Scriven 1967). As pointed out by Kelly (2008) or Drugan (2013), the overall tendency in T&I programmes has been to pay more attention to quality assessment (usually summative or normative) than to formative assessment and giving feedback to students, even if some innovative work in this area has been carried out by Dollerup (1994) and

Way (2006, 2008). I believe that formative evaluation strategies implemented in T&I courses would help both trainers and trainees to understand the process of learning and acquiring T&I skills and competence better, and that such knowledge would be essential for *practisearchers* in their practice, their research and their teaching.

4 Future directions

The main idea expounded in this book so far has been that the training of 21st century T&I professionals should be considered at the crossroads of practice, research and pedagogy. I have considered ways of bridging the gap between practice and research by providing more opportunities to practitioners to be more visible and pro-active and to find ways to be involved in research activities, as well as by exploring ways of teaching T&I trainees to better conceptualise practical questions through theory and through a better understanding of the knowledge-acquisition process. To conclude this discussion, I'd like to draw up some potential future directions which could facilitate these processes. As explained, training students to become practitioners-researchers – *practisearchers* – and recognising this status in higher education is, I believe, the best way to successfully bridge the gap between T&I practice and research. In trying to define how to train future *practisearchers*, I believe one should not forget to discuss the question of who should be in charge of such training and education. The idea that different approaches to research may facilitate the participation of practitioners in research projects has also been mentioned and therefore, I will also present here research approaches or models used in disciplines other than T&I Studies and which might be worth considering if one wants to encourage more research work to be developed on the basis of practice and experience.

4.1 Who should train future *practisearchers*?

I have already partly discussed the question of T&I trainers. I do not intend to repeat here what I have already said, but I will now present my views on who should be involved in the training and education of future *practisearchers* taking into account all the elements presented in this work.

With a view to proposing training aligned to industry and market needs (as suggested by Gouadec 2007 and Calvo 2011), institutions need to employ trainers who know the market and industry well and welcome their input into the curriculum (Mikkelson 2013). At the same time, running the risk of becoming too vocational is an issue for most universities which traditionally offer lectureships to staff with an academic background and publication records. What may therefore be needed 'is a harmonious combination of trainers who are primarily translators and trainers who are primarily academics' (Gouadec 2007, p. 354) or, even better, I would add, teachers who are both professionals and academics. It is in this perspective that I put forward the idea that *practisearchers* (tenured staff with both academic and professional backgrounds) would be the ideal T&I trainers and educators, if they were granted a recognised role in higher education. Recognition would be obtained on the premise that they conduct research and publish, but as important as their practice or research and publications may be, my view is that these practitioners-turned-into-researchers should also be required to be trained as T&I teachers.

I have already noted that being a T&I practitioner or/and a PhD holder does not make one a T&I teacher. As Setton (2010, p. 7) writes, 'it soon becomes obvious to any would-be-teacher, in any field, that understanding, doing and teaching are three different things', and therefore neither academics nor practitioners will become T&I trainers if they do not receive training in teaching. I wish to insist once more that training programmes in T&I and teams of instructors should be led by staff members with training and teaching experience and competence, and a good understanding of didactics (Hurtado Albir 2007; Kiraly 2000). Any T&I teaching staff member without this knowledge should be directed by one or two team leaders to undertake an induction period to understand the curriculum, the didactic tools used as well as the teaching philosophy and mindset of a particular programme and should be shown how research can gain from practice, how practice can gain from research, and how these gains can be turned into effective pedagogical tools to be implemented in the curriculum.

In a recent article on research in Interpreting Studies and the academisation of T&I programmes now set in academic environments – and I believe the comment can be extended to translator training –, Pöchhacker characterised today's situation on training as follows (2010, p. 5):

> The basic tenet of the training paradigm as articulated by Jennifer Mackintosh, i.e. that "the syllabus for consecutive and simultaneous interpretation should be designed and taught by practicing conference interpreters, preferably AIIC members", may still be valid, but is not necessarily sufficient for a university lectureship. AIIC itself has moved ahead in this regard, offering "Training the trainers" courses that,

with few exceptions, are still lacking within interpreter education institutions themselves, which should be expected to play a more prominent role in didactic development, given the increasing diversification of what is to be taught.

I would strongly echo the idea that T&I training and education is still lacking 'training-the-trainers' courses and that higher education institutions would be well advised to start considering training their teaching staff in the didactic specificities of T&I courses. The complexity of the vocational/academic divide issue requires that some effort be put into developing courses to clearly define a T&I teacher competence if the discipline wants to develop further in crossing that divide. I mentioned earlier a recent volume (Andres & Behr 2015) aiming at providing trainers with essential pedagogical knowledge about the didactics of conference interpreting training. As explained by the editors, the volume "does not aim to present in-depth scientific theories" but rather is "meant to serve as suggestions for experienced interpreter training practitioners who may not have received theory-based training in this domain during their training." It also "includes discussions on the relative usefulness of various exercise types as well as suggestions for making teaching in the days of short master's degree programmes even more efficient and student-oriented" (2015, p. 13). Further similar training-the-trainers initiatives, in all aspects of translation and interpreting training, would be welcome.

To blend practice, research and pedagogy in an efficient way, I believe that each programme should have one person/one team in charge of the curriculum and that he/she/they should know where they are heading, what objectives they want to achieve and how they can achieve them. Translation and interpreting jobs now involve such a multiplicity of tasks that training must be led by a director/a team familiar with all facets of the profession. A good knowledge of the industry markets is essential to understand why some pedagogical choices are made instead of others (Calvo 2011; Way 2008). In this respect, I would concur with Gouadec, who claims (2007, p. 355) that 'it is absolutely preposterous that academics can set up training programmes and pretend to train future translators without any first-hand personal experience of the profession [...] and without the slightest knowledge of market trends.' Academics should learn about current practice in the translation industry, about various tools and technologies used by professionals, and about professional strategies and techniques.

However, and as discussed at length already, knowing the profession but nothing of the academic discipline and the findings from the research carried out in T&I Studies will also be an impediment to the sound education of future *practisearchers*. Professionals involved in teaching should be informed about research trends, developments and methodologies in the discipline, and also be encouraged to engage in research activities and projects. They should be recommended to read articles published in academic journals, to attend symposia, workshops or conferences offered either in academia *per se* or by professional associations with professional development programmes.

Finally, both academics and practitioners should be invited to investigate and learn from research on T&I training and education in order to complement their academic and/or professional experience and intuition with a good understanding of key educational parameters such as learning, teaching and assessment competence.

It is not my intention to engage in an in-depth discussion of the teaching attributes that should be demanded and recognised in T&I education, but, in order to define (even broadly) a teacher competence profile, I wish to mention in particular the work carried out in this area by Dorothy Kelly. Using recent developments in this area in the UK, especially a higher education framework of standards for teachers as well as a White Paper on the future of higher education, Kelly (2008) delineated some teaching attributes for T&I teachers. Beyond T&I professional and academic knowledge, she distinguishes teaching skills as a 'central competence'. To define this competence, she then subdivides this competence into five main 'subcompetences' (2008, p. 105): organisational, interpersonal, instructional, contextual or professional, and finally instrumental. The components of the various 'subcompetences' are detailed in the table below in the form of desired abilities and skills to be possessed by teachers of any discipline. They constitute in my view relevant and essential attributes and areas of competence to consider when designing training-the-trainers courses in T&I training and education.

Organizational: the ability to design courses and appropriate teaching and learning activities   the ability to apply and manage these   the ability to design, apply and manage appropriate assessment activities
Interpersonal: the ability to work collaboratively with trainees towards their learning goals   the ability to work in a training team   the ability to act as a mentor for trainees
Instructional: the ability to present content and explain clearly   the ability to stimulate discussion and reflective thinking   the ability to arouse interest and enthusiasm
Contextual or professional: understanding of the educational context in which training takes place (local, national, international)   understanding of the teaching profession
Instrumental: knowledge of training resources of all kinds and ability to apply them appropriately and usefully to the training process

'Teaching Subcompetences' or areas of competence (Kelly 2008, pp. 105–106)

We know from educational theory that it is possible to conceive general guidelines for teacher training. In T&I training and education, beyond their knowledge of the profession and the discipline, any conscientious teacher will need to learn to explain how T&I skills and knowledge acquisition work and why students stumble on this or that hurdle during their training (Gabr 2007; Kearns 2006; Robinson 2003). To gain that ability, T&I staff must be introduced to pedagogical theories and to the notions of course design, progression and students' learning curves; they should be trained in classroom techniques, in grading and assessment procedures and especially feedback techniques, and they need to understand the whole pedagogical project of the curriculum. I consider the above-mentioned standards proposed by Kelly to be in line with such objectives. Given that the task of teaching is a complex and multi-faceted one, if teachers are familiar with the curriculum and adhere to its underpinnings, they will become more confident and efficient in their teaching methods. As Setton notes (2010, p. 10), it must never be forgotten that

> teachers navigate a space between two constraining 'guiderails': on one side, the fixed rail of the course structure and progression, with its defined steps, exercises and intermediate objectives (and parallel language and knowledge development), and on the other, the variable paces and styles of the different individual students, allowing for plateaux, leaps and dips, which may also call for occasional 'morale management'.

T&I staff members' teaching and practice should be based both on their ability to reflect on their subject and their own competence in the field. This is where the metacognitive approach I discussed earlier may become valuable: if future *practisearchers* are aware of the learning processes involved in the acquisition of T&I skills and competence, they will easily gain the ability to translate their experience and knowledge in a training course, if they decide to be involved in T&I teaching.

In making recommendations on the way to train trainers and educators, Gouadec noted that T&I trainers' positions 'must be filled by people who have all the necessary academic accomplishments as well as a perfect knowledge of the conditions, processes, constraints and tools prevalent in the translation industry. Each trainer must therefore be perfectly at home on both sides of the fence' (2007, p. 356). I have tried to show in this sub-section that such a view is incomplete to me and that it is crucial to consider a third facet of the practitioner-researcher's identity if we want to see the practice and research gap bridged: that of the teacher.

It is important to note that to have a chance of seeing theory and research findings fully considered and integrated into training – and then flow into practice through the communicating vessels principle – theory and research must be internalised in the T&I curriculum and in its procedures, but more importantly well-communicated to, and adhered to, by the teaching staff who would be in charge of passing on knowledge, concepts and notions.

Finding and motivating teaching *practisearchers* and trainers of future *practisearchers* will not be an easy task. Setting up training-the-trainers courses along the lines described above will not be an easy exercise. Implementing strategies whereby teaching staff have the possibility of practising professionally, conducting research and undertaking teacher training will inevitably be costly. However, I believe that with a view to establishing a sustainable benchmark in quality T&I training and education, and facilitating more natural links between T&I practice, research and training, T&I training institutions will have to seriously consider such options.

To conclude, I would like to raise an issue related to the future of T&I training. Interestingly, in his recommendations on training, Gouadec (2007, p. 356) added the following to his previous comment:

> Failing that, the fence will remain a barrier between the academic world and the profession/industry and actual translator training will inevitably take place outside the universities. Academic translator trainers have to meet the challenge or run the risk to see training outsourced to private companies.

I have not discussed in great detail this idea that, should higher education institutions decide not to recognise the status of *practisearchers* in certain disciplines, they would indeed run the risk of seeing training taken over by private industry-based companies or institutes which would expect young graduates to be job-ready and to respond to precise industrial requirements. It is my firm belief that if *practisearchers* as I have defined them are tomorrow's T&I trainers and educators, this threat should only remain a threat.

4.2 Could a practice-informed research approach constitute an acceptable model for academic recognition of T&I practice?

To conclude this chapter, I would like to deal with an idea that I have alluded to several times. I have argued that if practitioners and trainees were enabled to conduct or be involved in research projects, the T&I community would be able to see more experiential and practical knowledge turned into academic and educational material. I have also indicated that disciplines in other areas (e.g. the visual and performing arts, music, theatre, creative writing) have recently developed research paradigms and models which allow them to turn their practice into research outputs. I would like therefore to consider if such paradigms and models could be applicable to T&I Studies. Should these models be recognised as convenient research tools in T&I, interactions and synergies between the professional and the academic may be facilitated.

Hale and Napier (2013) define research as searching for new knowledge in a systematic, organised way. Research questions will be addressed by choosing an appropriate methodology which can strictly follow a specific paradigm, such as quantitative or qualitative, or can use mixed methods. As they also stress, research can 'confirm or disconfirm other sources of knowledge' and 'new research will also often contribute to new research methodologies – to how to conduct research in more effective, efficient, innovative and valid ways' (2013, p. 5).

On researching a particular object or phenomenon, the first stage to be covered is that of choosing a research model. To do this, Beeby recommends that we 'identify the object to be investigated and the reason for studying it' (2000, p. 44). Since the T&I field is characterised by the multiplicity of its facets, determining what object and problem to study when conducting research in T&I Studies is a complex issue. As far as a methodology of research for T&I Studies is concerned, one should of course bear in mind that T&I Studies as an independent discipline is very young and that 'its object of study is complex and approachable in many different ways' (Cravo 2007, p. 92). Because of the wealth and complexity of the field, the discipline has struggled to exist and to find an identity beyond the traditional fields of literary studies, cultural studies or linguistics. There has been quite extensive debate within the discipline concerning ways of defining the means and methodologies to better analyse its complex object (objects?) of study, and 'these ongoing debates serve to prove that there must be a place for new methods and methodologies for there is much still to be studied and better understood' (Cravo 2007, p. 92).

The point made by Cravo, as well as by Hale and Napier, is that there seems to be room in T&I Studies for innovative methodologies and approaches. Cravo, for example, advocates the use of *action research*. Action research can be classified as a sub-area under the banner of applied research (i.e. more descriptive research with generally immediate practical use), and can be defined as 'research conducted by practitioners, designed to solve real-life problems that affect the researcher/practitioner' (Hale & Napier 2013, p. 11). Practitioners would generally present critical case study analysis of their own work and 'engage in cyclical, reflective analysis of a key problem' (2013, p. 114). In T&I Studies, several authors have referred to the use of action research in their activities (Cravo 2007; Hatim 2001; Kiraly 2000), and Cravo (2007, p. 93) argues that

> action research can play an important role in [Translation Studies]. Issues that have not been explained, practices that have not been described, bridges between scholars and practitioners that have not yet been crossed, gaps between theory and practice that remain to be covered, may be dealt with through AR.

Attempts to carry out research on practical work have also been termed 'interpreter fieldwork research', in the case of interpreting, and can be considered as a form of autoethnography (Starfield 2010): 'a blend of autobiography and ethnography' (Hale & Napier 2013, p. 114).

On the basis of these observations, action research appears as a viable research model to carry out investigations on experiential and practical topics to solve a problem and provide answers to the profession. I agree that this methodology should indeed be considered by practitioners-researchers and that it seems perfectly suitable for T&I Studies. As explained, action research can be seen as a sub-branch of applied research and would generally follow the qualitative paradigm to provide a solution to an identified *problem*. However, in other disciplines, and in particular in the creative arts, the concept of carrying out research from the identification of a problem is not always a valid one. Various practice-informed models may consider a different starting point to justify the conduct of research activities (Biggs 2000).

Practice-led research, for example, does not stem from the sense of a problem but from the experience itself. Practice-led research is concerned with the nature of practice and leads to new knowledge that has operational significance for that practice (Candy 2006). The approach focuses on the practical experience, which becomes to a certain extent the object being studied and analysed, a model which 'holds that practice is the principal research activity [...] and sees the material outcomes of practice as all-important representations of research findings in their own right' (Haseman 2006, p. 7). In his 2006 manifesto for practice-led research, Haseman – a noted researcher in the visual arts – stated (2006, p. 1):

> Researchers in the arts, media and design often struggle to find serviceable methodologies within the orthodox research paradigms of quantitative and qualitative research. In response to this and over the past decade, practice-led research has emerged as a potent strategy for those researchers who wish to initiate and then pursue their research through practice.

As clearly stated in his piece, quantitative and qualitative research practices are two different methods of research, arising from fundamentally different views of the world. They embody alternative understandings of how knowledge is created. With practice-led research however, predicting the research path is difficult. 'The linking of experience, practice and theory to produce situated knowledge, knowledge that operates in relation to established knowledge' (Barrett 2007, p. 145) often demands that the researcher look beyond traditional models as the research is situated in a field of inquiry.

Historically, quantitative research has been seen as the most solid method and qualitative as a 'softer', more tentative one. But, as Haseman put it, 'how are these research practices applied to the study of meaning-making practices generally, those involving "the actual application of a plan or method, as opposed to the theories relating to it" (OECD)?' (2006, p. 2). In other words, Haseman suggests that these two approaches might not be sufficient or may be too restrictive for certain disciplines, especially as they place emphasis only on 'written outcomes' and distort the 'communication of practice' that some disciplines express. The impatience of some researchers has thus motivated a radical push not only to 'place practice within the research process but to lead research through practice' (2006, p. 3). By definition, practice-led research would then be purely experiential and would create 'new forms for performance and exhibition'. In my view, T&I Studies could fall under this definition. Using T&I experience as communicative performance (even if written in the case of translation) to lead research can be seen as highly relevant if one agrees on the fact that such practice-led research does not start with a sense of a problem but more from an 'enthusiasm of practice'

(Haseman 2006, p. 5) and is individual and idiosyncratic. The starting point is the experience itself, which can be triggered by a new form of technology, a new context, a new query from a client/end-user, and from which practice follows. I contend that such an approach would make great sense in regards to T&I publications based on experiences which triggered a reflection on practice and the development of new knowledge, and would certainly be welcomed by other T&I *practisearchers* who do not find in the research models current in their own institutions the pathway to turn their experience into research.

The concept of *practice-as-research* (a variant of practice-led research) is growing internationally and 'there is a burgeoning literature on practice-as-research to reflect an international and spreading phenomenon with strong established or emergent movements of postdoctoral or postgraduate practitioners-researchers' (Nelson 2013, p. 4). The concept and activity, which has a history spanning about two decades and is well established in various countries such as Australia, the UK, South Africa, France, Canada or the Nordic countries (Nelson 2013) entails 'practical knowledge which might primarily be demonstrated in practice – that is, knowledge which is a matter of doing rather than abstractly conceived, and thus able to be articulated by way of a traditional thesis in words alone' (2013, p. 9). The concept of practical knowledge underpinning the approach is that a practitioner may be doing something without necessarily being able to explain why and how he/she is doing it. A simple example to understand practical knowledge is that of knowing how to ride a bicycle.

> I know how to ride a bicycle but I cannot say how I balance because I have no method. I may know that certain muscles are involved, but that factual knowledge comes later, if at all, and it could hardly be used in instruction. To know how to ride a bicycle is to ride it. (Philosopher David Pears, cited in Nelson 2013, p. 9)

As for practice-led research, practice-as-research may appeal to T&I practitioners who wish to engage in research as such research arises where an insightful practice is submitted as a substantial part of the evidence of a research inquiry. Many T&I projects could certainly become research projects if the discipline embraced the approach as other disciplines have.

With the aim of seeing more and more practical knowledge and professional intuitions turned into research projects and enriching the literature in T&I Studies and T&I training, I would recommend to T&I practitioners that they seriously consider any of the approaches briefly described here. Opting for such approaches does not mean that qualitative or quantitative models will not be used afterwards, but the initial idea would stem from practice and experience and be individual. I also believe efforts should be made in training institutions to teach students how to use these various research models. Should trainees/future *practisearchers* be taught about different methodologies and paradigms (quantitative, qualitative and practice-informed) from the beginning of their T&I training, they may be more inclined to engage in research projects when they become practitioners if they do not feel intimidated by research models. Moreover, I personally believe that the way research is presently undertaken may be acting as a barrier to engagement with stakeholders from the industry, and I would argue that a practice-informed approach, based on practical knowledge, might facilitate greater involvement with the sector and the broader vocational community too.

The literature on such practice-informed approaches to research (i.e. action research, practice-led research, practice-as-research) is full of case studies which show the diversity and richness of practice as research projects (e.g. Biggs 2000; Candy 2006; Colbert 2009; Nelson 2013), but it does not provide a research methodology distinguishing the approach of practitioners-researchers nor does it offer an exemplary pedagogy to support the development of new *practisearchers*. I hope that somehow this book and the suggestions made will play a role in the effort to fill this gap.

5   Case studies and examples

This part of the book will focus on examples which will illustrate what was discussed in the previous part: the idea to use knowledge gained through practical experience and turn it into research questions and activities which can lead to the implementation of pedagogical activities in a training curriculum which aims at preparing future T&I professionals for the realities and requirements of their profession. The examples chosen are based on various insights gained through my personal practice of interpreting or translating that I used to design pedagogical activities to be implemented in the classroom. The main driver was my intention to use professional practice and experience, or my knowledge of standards and normative practices in the profession as well as in T&I education and, after conducting research projects or gathering literature reviews and reflections on similar research areas, to develop pedagogical and training tools to train future professionals to acquire new skills and practical awareness, which could be adopted in professional practice.

The first two examples deal with interpreting, the last one with translation. The first example is a reflection on how interpreting practice can influence training and practice, stemming from an assignment in which I had to interpret for a French author during several sessions of a Writers' Festival. The experience triggered reflections on my practice as a consecutive interpreter, as it became clear to me during the assignment that interpreting for a writer could be a different exercise to interpreting for a politician or a scientist. The second relates to the way new technological advances, namely *digital pen technology*, can influence interpreter training, research and practice. It illustrates how the synergies between technology/pedagogy, research, and then practice, can lead to interesting developments in the profession. They show how being exposed to technological novelties in a pedagogical environment can lead to new discoveries, new training practices, new research, and can potentially help the profession to develop further and move towards new directions. This case study presents the technology and its use in the interpreting field and suggests pedagogical activities to be implemented in note-taking and consecutive interpreting. It also focuses on a comparative study of the use of the technology in a hybrid mode of interpreting which bore interesting results in terms of accuracy, fluency and comfort. Introducing the hybrid mode in interpreting training is also discussed.

The example about translation deals with the complex topic of assessment of quality in translation. It presents pedagogical tools used in a postgraduate course aimed at taking into account both product- and process-oriented evaluation approaches. The idea put forward is that, in an increasingly complex professional environment, in which it is possible to work in various contexts and geographical areas with distinct assessment norms, it is paramount to make trainees aware of future clients' or end-users' practices and expectations but also to enable them to reflect on the translational process in their own practice.

5.1 Literary interpreting

This illustration of the way experience can inform pedagogy and practice again later on arose from an assignment where I had to interpret for a writer during a four-day writers' festival and realised that the act of interpreting in this context implied different strategies in the practice of consecutive interpreting. As stated earlier in this book, the diversification of contexts of work today often obliges interpreters to adapt their skills to the specificities of the setting and to apply different working modalities. Interpreting in literature festivals may be considered as belonging to the field of media interpreting, an environment that does not 'fall neatly into the broad, conventional categories of interpreting' (Mead 2012, p. 172). If one considers interpreting settings of work as 'a conceptual spectrum' (Pöchhacker 2002) ranging from international conferences at one end to community interpreting at the other, media interpreting would be difficult to categorise as it bears characteristics entailed by the international nature of the assignment but 'is essentially set within the institutional context of a specific socio-cultural community and is therefore community-based as well as international' (Pöchhacker 2004, p. 162). Interpretations in such an unusual setting may therefore impose unusual modalities on the interpreter, who may have to mobilise skills in an unusual way. The personal experience gained during this assignment triggered some questions which led me to believe that different working modalities in consecutive interpreting may need to be considered when interpreting in such a setting, and later on when training future interpreters.

In consecutive interpreting with notes, interpreters are usually trained to 'discard the words' of the original and 'convey the sense of various units of meaning' (Seleskovitch, 1975), and to focus their note-taking conventions on 'ideas, not words' (Rozan, 1956). I believe, however, that interpreting for a writer requires a different approach, since nothing is more important to a writer than words.

During the Auckland Writers' Festival 2007, I had the privilege to interpret for Andrei Makine, the celebrated French writer of Russian origin. Apart from the assignment itself, the particular interest I found in this task, was that I had to interpret the words of a writer while he was being asked to reflect upon his work and the processes of creation, writing, and translation; a different content to what I would usually do at the time. I believe that the work I had to perform revealed a new facet of the complex work of the interpreter for I could not rely on the interpreting techniques I usually use. Reading my notes afterwards and reflecting on this special assignment, I came to the conclusion that interpreting for a writer – would it be true for any artist? – is different from the usual kind of work an interpreter does.

I prepared for the assignment as thoroughly as I could. I was provided with a lot of information about Mr. Makine. I was sent the questions which would be asked to the writer and the themes which would be talked about. I read many interviews with Mr. Makine from which I gained the clear impression that he is someone who does not want or like people to be able to anticipate his responses. And when I met him for the first time, and asked him after a while if we could read through the questions and prepare the events, he simply rejected the idea, albeit in a very friendly manner, explaining that he loved improvisation, and that he would not know until the precise moment of the question what he would answer. Too many elements – the place, the public, the atmosphere – would influence his reflexions. Mr. Makine has little knowledge of English, but during the first event, within ten minutes, he realised that I was not translating *exactly* what he had just said. He realised I was translating the idea, not the words. He therefore asked me to interpret, or to try to interpret, all his words, and he also wanted the audience to be informed about this demand. Consequently, I realised that I could not simply try to codify his words and transmit only the message, the idea: the notes I was taking had to be more extensive and be more literal. Not only did I try to deliver the meaning of his message, but I also tried to translate the words, almost all the words, and to convey to the audience Makine's very distinctive spirit, soul and style.

The task was unusual and different; certainly less mechanical. I produced more than a verbal translation, more than an interpretation. I soon realised that I was more concerned than usual with the audience's understanding of and reaction to what was being said. Makine speaks as creatively as he writes, and I was wondering if the *epiphanies* he mentioned, the *aporias* he talked about, the poetic tone, images and style he deployed – his eloquence – were all understood and felt as they should be. And I did not want the audience to miss any of the particularities of what this artist was saying (rather cryptically at times) about the process of creation and writing, or about his feelings of loss and fulfilment regarding the act of translating, or even to miss his tendency to create a progressive effect when addressing important questions. Like many artists, Mr. Makine is a performer, and you can feel that he likes performing. He also wanted to be funny and to amuse the audience. This also had to be translated. All translators know that the translation of humour is a very difficult and dangerous exercise. But in order to keep the spirit of Mr. Makine's words, and also to transmit his desire to be funny and entertain the public, the mere translation of ideas would not have worked. Everything he said, with an emphasis on certain specific words, had to be relayed.

As I wrote nearly the whole of what Mr. Makine was saying, I ended up with quite long and dense *literary* passages to translate. It was as if I was performing a sight translation. More precisely in this case, I was producing a *literary* sight translation. This was rather unusual too. Following the principle that the interpreter should capture only the idea, relay the gist of what is being said, I was doing a very bad job. But if one admits that it was ethically, linguistically and artistically important to relay the exact style and spirit of Makine's words, then my unusually detailed notes – where nearly every word had its importance – were justified.

Simultaneous interpretation would surely be a better option when interpreters have to work on such assignments, but the logistic and economic demands it requires will make it impossible for festival organisers to consider it. Yet the job has to be performed. Interpreters have to be aware of this facet of their work and have to be prepared and trained to focus, on certain occasions, as much on words as on ideas. No doubt I worked differently on that occasion; I had to be more creative than usual and to use linguistic *and* literary skills. I found the resources to do so in my own literary background. Was it a requirement to perform well that day? I don't know. But the work I did was definitely of a stylistic, literary order.

The main purpose of my reflection after this assignment was to propose and discuss the possible existence of a new facet in interpreting, that of *literary interpreting*, whereby the interpreter, when interpreting for an artist, may have to put the focus of the note-taking and the rendering as much on words as on ideas. Just as literary translation is different from technical and legal translation, *literary interpreting* could be seen as different from court or diplomatic interpreting.

Following on those reflections on the assignment, I wrote an article on the topic (Orlando 2010a). After its publication in the AALITRA journal, I was asked by AIIC, the International Association of Conference Interpreters, if the article could be published on their online magazine. They liked the idea that interpreting for a writer could bear some unique specificities and thought the article would be of interest to their readership of professional conference interpreters, as many work for literary or art festivals. The article was published in their Winter 2011 issue, and was then made available to a wider community of practitioners. A few weeks after the issue was released, I received the following email from a Germany-based conference interpreter who had been working for many years in the field of literature, theatre and the arts and thanked me for having brought up the question. She confirmed that, to her, working in those fields was not a usual exercise:

> I love the challenge and – since I have met many writers and filmmakers, photographers and painters in my career – the diversity of interpreting modes you're required to adopt in this particular setting. And it's almost always 'consec', as you point out. Some writers are eloquent, some are shy, some are vain, some are modest, some are drunk (yes, it happens, and it does not enhance their intelligibility), some hosts know how to ask questions, some don't seem to know what they want to know. Sometimes the audience loves you (the interpreter) too, sometimes the artist/writer does not want the audience to love anybody except the artist/writer, yet

they depend on you (the interpreter) to get the message across. (2011, personal correspondence with L.A G).

Even though this testimony cannot be taken as representative of interpreters' views of what interpretations in such settings entail, I believe it is an informative and insightful contribution for further considerations on the topic of literary interpreting in relation to literary translation and the other settings of interpreting work.

The article was also the source of an academic publication by Peter Mead (2012), who discussed the topic of interpreting during a literary festival in Italy, in which he has worked as an interpreter for more than a decade. Even though his data analysis and conclusions do not fully support the addition of a new facet in the taxonomy of interpreting, Mead pointed out that 'Orlando's description of "literary interpreting" [...] can be appreciated as a contribution to the growing awareness of working modalities and environments which do not fall neatly into the conventional categories of interpreting' (2012, p. 172). Further, Mead states that 'even if comments focusing on features of literary language do not occur very often in my experience of interpreting for authors, metalinguistic comment is quite frequent. [...] This obviously does require the level of attention to words and nuances of which Marc Orlando speaks' (p. 177). In conclusion, Mead adds that his 'perception is that "the literary interpreting" genre is on the increase' (p. 182).

This new notion led me to envisage training recommendations using theoretical views and perspectives on consecutive interpreting and literary translation; a relevant illustration of the way questions arising from practice can be considered and investigated in relation to the literature on the topic and turned into didactic elements. Because of the importance of training future interpreters to be able to adapt to various environments, and because the *literary interpreting* genre may indeed be on the increase, I investigated the T&I literature on subjects like types of settings, types of source speech, and types of rendition (Gile 1995; Pöchhacker 2002, 2004; Seleskovitch 1975, 1984/2001) and implemented in particular a series of exercises which were introduced in the consecutive interpreting classroom of our T&I program and aimed to make trainees aware that interpreting is not an automatic act.

When analysing speeches Seleskovitch (1975) distinguishes three distinct forms (descriptive, dialectic and affective) to which three forms of interpretation correspond (an explanation, an argumentation, and an eloquence exercise). According to her, each form implies a more or less 'deverbalised' interpretation and, when interpreting, the interpreter will have to be more or less faithful to the words of the source speech. Following on such categorisation and elaborating on Seleskovitch's suggestions, I introduced reflections on and activities for consecutive interpretation from texts which allowed the following distinctions: The explanatory, descriptive interpretation (e.g. technical or scientific debates, procedural discussions), totally devoid of emotive power, can be longer or shorter than the original, and also very free as far as reformulation is concerned. The most important is that the stream of thought is perfectly conveyed and understood. The meaning is what matters, and the content of the interpretation prevails even if its form differs from the original. The argumentative interpretation (e.g. political negotiations, arbitration tribunals, where the stances of the participants are known beforehand) must scrupulously reflect the original speech and all the nuances of the words and terms chosen, as well as convey all the arguments and intentions of the speaker (threat, limitation, compromise, etc). Both content and form matter with such an interpretation. An eloquent speech, however, (e.g. welcome opening remarks, thank-you dinner or banquet speeches) is generally targeted at an audience, not at interlocutors. It aims at moving the audience and at triggering off emotions. When interpreting eloquence, the interpreter has to convey the same emotions, feelings and style, and therefore has to make a connection with the audience and find the right voice. During an eloquence exercise, the form is preponderant. Obviously, one speech can be a mix of those different forms and the role of the interpreter is to always be absolutely and totally faithful to the speaker.

Despite the artificial character of such distinctions, I believe it is relevant to train interpreters in the different methods of interpretation they imply. These exercises have been designed to show students that analysing the speech content in the light of the proposed distinctions would help them to render the source speech as comprehensively, faithfully and eloquently as possible. Using my personal experience during the interpretations for Andrei Makine and the directions suggested by T&I scholars, as well as comments from other interpreters working in such settings, has been an invaluable asset when setting up these pedagogical tools.

Finally, to conclude on this topic, I would like to mention a training session which was organised by and took place at the University of Mainz in Germany in June 2013, and involving the Faculty of Translation Studies, Linguistics and Cultural Studies based in Germersheim. Using the potential new facet of interpreting described above, I was invited to chair a working session with students from the departments of Interpreting Studies and of Translation Studies on the relations between literary translation and literary interpreting. Using different literary texts and writers' interviews, translators were invited to provide written translations and interpreters to deliver oral interpretations, and then differences and similarities in approaches were discussed with all the participants. Based on these exchanges and on the views of the (literary) translators present during the session, the audience of interpreters concluded that literary interpreting would be an interesting concept to investigate further, as it was recognised that the act of interpreting was unusual and different, and that such text types would require different strategies on the part of the interpreter.

I see these various reactions to the new concept of *literary interpreting* (comments from AIIC colleagues, publications by other scholars on the topic, attempts to assess the relation between literary translation and interpreting) as positive signs showing that the assumptions drawn from a professional assignment may be considered as new knowledge and are worth further investigation. It would be really invaluable and very fruitful to invite other practitioners to provide information and their reflection on their practice and to try to turn their experience into potential research and training material.

5.2 Digital pen technology

This example will present and discuss the use of digital pen technology in the interpreting classroom, especially applied to consecutive interpreting and note-taking training, but also to professional practice and research.

In 2009, during a technology seminar on how new technologies could influence language education, I was introduced to new technology, the Livescribe digital pen, whose advanced features allow its users to record and capture simultaneously what they write in relation to what is said in the room. The device was originally invented to assist secretaries in their taking of minutes during meetings and in retrieving their notes, and has since been trialled and used for research projects in various fields such as education, engineering, health and allied health, or science (e.g. Boyle 2012; Dawson & Plummer 2010; Greeve & McGee-Lennon 2010).

5.2.1 Digital pen technology and note-taking training

Immediately inspired by the device and its unique features, I proceeded to trial it in the note-taking classroom for consecutive interpreting. Most research in the field of note-taking had so far focussed only on the interpreter's notes as a *product*, rarely on the *process* of note-taking; the main reason being the limitations of the available technology and resources. When instructors want to assess an interpretation, it is generally the quality of the consecutive interpretation (based on criteria to evaluate the linguistic accuracy, as well as their expression and presentation) and the final notes (the product) which allow them to give feedback and evaluate the performance. Such a *product* evaluation of the interpretation is generally made without being able to clearly distinguish the memorisation qualities or deficiencies and the note-taking qualities or deficiencies of the interpreter. One possibility to evaluate the note-taking *process* (the significance of notes being taken 'live') is to find a way to capture simultaneously the notes and the speech. To do so, some instructors have for example used OHPs and transparent paper or have asked students to use the classroom board. The capture of the note-taking process has also been done by video-recording the interpreter at work and by comparing the recording with the speech from which notes were taken. It is worth mentioning as an example the large and invaluable empirical study on note-taking conducted by Dörte Andres (2002), where one could really follow the note-taking process of 14 students and 14 professional interpreters. Each of them was video-recorded taking notes from a speech and rendering the speech, and Andres painstakingly noted the exact second when each element was spoken in the original, appeared in the note-pad, and was spoken by the interpreter. The script of the original speech and that of the interpretation were put together on the same sheet of paper, with the notes in between to allow the visualisation of the links and the evaluation of qualities and defects. It seems that no similar study has been repeated since. However, weekly and all over the world, instructors lead workshops on consecutive interpretation and note-taking techniques, where students' performances and notes are assessed. Unfortunately, the time and resources required prevent most trainers from repeating the colossal work done by Andres, and from analysing the quality of the interpretations in relation to the note-taking process. In most training programs, this results in the incapacity and impossibility to provide well-considered and personalised remedial strategies to improve the students' skills, based on their personal learning.

Digital pens belong to the category of mobile computing platforms. They offer advanced processing power, audio and visual feedback, and memory for handwriting capture, audio recording, and additional applications. The *Smartpen* consists of a microphone, a built-in speaker, 3D recording headsets, and an infrared camera. It is used to take notes—it has a normal ink cartridge and is held like a normal pen—and to capture data on a microchipped paper. Thanks to the built-in microphone and speaker and the infrared camera, an application synchronises what is being filmed/recorded as handwriting with the audio recording. Thanks to the *dot-paper* technology, which enables interactive "live" capture using plain paper printed with microdots, and to a function called Paper Replay, the user of the pen can play back the speech from the notes made on paper at any time. One simply needs to tap on a word on the page of the notebook to hear the part of the speech related to that same word or a phrase played directly from the pen. For better comfort in listening, the flow of the audio playback can also be slowed down or sped up as required. It is possible to connect the first generations of *Smartpens* to a computer through a normal USB port so that both audio and video data can be uploaded and played on the computer. This allows users to back up, search, and replay notes from their computer. Users can also upload and convert notes to interactive Flash movies or pdf files. The latest model of the *Smartpen* is wireless, enabling instant transfer of what has been written down to any playback device (e.g., computer, tablet, iPad, smart phone, etc.).

With its unique technical features allowing the simultaneous recording of both what is said in the room and what is written by the user, the pen offers for the first time ever the possibility to capture *live* the process of note-taking of an interpreter at work. As the data can be uploaded on any type of computer and be turned into different formats, it offers, in the classroom, the possibility of projecting the notes of trainees and discussing them as a classroom activity and, combined with other technologies, pinpointing the qualities and defects of the notes in relation to the source speech and the interpretation. As far as the learning process of note taking is concerned, research suggests that the use of text-to-speech technology and effective note-taking activities, coupled with review, can aid learning and understanding and therefore enhance the comprehension, fluency, accuracy, speed, endurance, and concentration of individuals (Tran & Lawson, 2001; Lindstrom, 2007). One can thus consider that if the taking of notes is too demanding on a student's working memory to permit the student to carry out generative processing in real time and, in the case of interpreting students, leads to a poor performance, the needed generative processing of the content can still occur during the follow-up review of notes. Given the difficulties many students face when reading their own notes, the synchronous juxtaposition of text and audio provided by this digital pen technology should induce greater learning from the students when reading, reviewing and evaluating their own notes during assessment activities. Moreover, during these self-, peer-, or class-assessment activities, such technology enables students and instructors to work together closely and clearly observe and/or show what can be noted down or not, what notes are useful or not, what is detrimental to the restitution, and so on. It allows all of the participants to make an objective evaluation of what constitutes economic and effective notes.

In 2009, I started developing pedagogical sequences using the *Smartpen* to help trainers to find new personalised and efficient process-oriented remediation strategies (Orlando 2010b) in which a formative metacognitive approach prevails. In any institution training future professionals, no one would contest the benefit of evaluating students against various professional standards. Our programme, for example, is approved by the National Accreditation Authority for Translators and Interpreters (NAATI) and is therefore subject to monitoring and controls aiming at ensuring that our evaluation principles follow and comply with NAATI professionally-oriented standards and principles. And it is a good thing to focus on product, professional-oriented assessment objectives, especially towards the end of the training period. However, as pointed out by Choi (2006), such professional focus and evaluation also runs the risk of defeating the purpose of evaluation and assessment from a pedagogical standpoint. Therefore, it is important for assessment to be studied also from the student's perspective. Self-assessment and metacognition play an important part when one wants to give students the possibility to reflect on their progress, to 'learn how to learn' and to become actors in their own learning process. As defined by Choi, 'metacognition in learning can be described as the awareness of the learning process and the ability to adapt to challenges that occur during this process through effective strategies, thereby helping learners improve their learning capacity' (Choi 2006, p. 277).

The activities I developed aimed at trialling the technology as a resource to facilitate students' evaluation of their own note-taking conventions, and were introduced in the second semester of our three-semester Masters programme, at a point where trainees had already established a foundation and gained a clear understanding of the nature of consecutive interpretation and at a point where they had also developed their own system of note-taking. In order to collect data on students' progress and feedback on the assessment of notes using the captured handwriting and speech, the following steps were undertaken to ensure that all students and educators had the same exposure to the digital pen in the classroom. They were requested to follow the sequence described below when working on the consecutive interpretation of speeches. The sequence was set up for a group class activity (up to 6 students). Each student in the group was provided with a *Smartpen*. The instructor used a video camera to film the students' performance.

Class activity

Step 1: The speech to be interpreted is played or read to students who take notes with their digital pen (the speech is audio recorded and the notes are filmed thanks to the pen's infrared camera).

Step 2: The instructor asks the students one after the other to provide their interpretation of one part of the speech and video records them.

Step 3: One student's filmed interpretation is video projected and assessed by the group in terms of communication quality (body language, voice, style etc.) and accuracy (the written version of the source speech is provided to the students and missing or misinterpreted elements are noted and listed down).

Step 4: The information recorded by this student's pen (speech and notes) is played on a computer, a laptop or an iPad and is projected to the class. The instructor and students focus on the 'live' filmed notes and on the list of misinterpreted or missing elements, and try to identify potential reasons in the process of note-taking to explain the deficiencies. This step is repeated for each student and each part of the speech.

Step 5: A general discussion is conducted by the instructor, stressing the importance of a collective evaluation and of cross-student feedback about the difference performances and note-taking conventions. Comments and ideas are shared based on the notes assessed during the session.

As the collected data can be turned into a flash movie or a PDF document, students were invited to upload their notes on a USB key at the end of each workshop for further use. Alternatively, they could ask their instructor to send it to them by email, for further self-assessment. At the end of the semester, a questionnaire was distributed to all students. The main objective of the questionnaire was to check how students perceive the impact of the digital pen on their note-taking conventions, and to record their views on the use of the *Smartpen* during their training in consecutive interpreting. Based on the responses of students and educators (see below), it is my belief that the treatment and review of all data on a weekly basis added to the assessment of the interpreter's performance either by the instructor, by a peer, or on a self-assessment basis, undoubtedly helps to identify patterns useful to define personal remedial strategies in the learning process.

As expressed previously in this book (see 3.3.3.2), metacognitive strategies assist students in their learning process, helping them to understand how to learn (metacognitive knowledge) and, through feedback mechanisms, how to develop remediation strategies (metacognitive skills). Feedback is therefore at the centre of any metacognitive and student-centred approach (Veenman 2006). Thanks to the digital pen technology, interpreter trainees are able to self-assess their work but also to assess their peers and to develop personalised remedies to their note-taking problems in consecutive interpreting through this cross-fertilisation. This evaluation of their work in a process-oriented formative approach should help them to improve their performance in consecutive interpreting with notes and to be better prepared to cope with the reality of their profession.

I would like now to make a specific mention of another instance of implementation of the technology in training. In June 2013, I was the recipient of the Gutenberg Teaching Council grant at the University of Mainz/Germersheim in Germany. I was invited there for two weeks to assist the Interpreting Studies programme to implement the digital pen technology in their course and to present the tool to their staff members and students. Different induction sessions were organised to show how the digital pen can be used in the classroom for note-taking activities and feedback, and both students and educators had the opportunity to test and use its features through one of the pedagogical sequences mentioned above. I decided then to survey both students and staff members from Mainz/Germersheim University and also from Monash University by means of a questionnaire, and to present their responses in a comparative analysis which was published in an edited volume on approaches to teaching conference interpreting (Orlando 2015b). To show how interpreter training can benefit from digital pen technology, I would like to briefly present some of the results of the survey. The questionnaire focused on the general usability of the pen and the play-back functions and effects on note-taking analysis, and the overall benefit to the development of good note-taking conventions including cross-student feedback.

The responses from the students of both universities reveal that despite the fact that they have been trained in note-taking for at least a semester, and that some problems have already been identified and discussed with them, many still discover issues with their notes when using the pen and playing back their notes.

They also mention several positive elements in having the possibility to see their notes projected. The possibility offered to observe the lag between the speech and the notes in real-time is by far the most appreciated, followed by a clear identification of what they do not understand or memorise properly. Students seem therefore well aware of the need to have access to the process of notes being taken in order to identify their personal defects and determine personalised remediation strategies. Using the pen and viewing playbacks also makes some of them aware of necessary changes and possible areas of improvement. Viewing playbacks of other students was judged profitable by the majority of informants. Most of them mentioned getting better ideas and tips from others for symbols, layout and links. Globally, students find advantages in using the pen during their workshops, especially in having the possibility to identify and better analyse problems. The responses confirm what was already put forward after previous informal experiments: there is merit in introducing the use of the digital pen in the classroom at some stage in the training curriculum, as part of a metacognitive strategy. The pen's features enable students to visualize and identify better their own qualities or deficiencies, to share ideas and get inspiration from other students, to understand better and analyse what can go wrong if they take excessive or disorganised notes.

As for the educators, responses were collected from eight Germersheim and five Monash educators. All respondents are both practitioners and educators. They all teach consecutive interpreting and offer comment on their students' note-taking conventions during their classes. Most of the responses provided are in line with the views of all other trainers who have tried using the pen for pedagogical reasons and with whom I have had the opportunity to have informal exchanges. With this sample of 13 educators, no specific difference relative to their respective institutions was apparent. Most of them indicated the same issues when teaching consecutive interpreting and note-taking: students focus too much on their systems of notes and write too much; they do not listen to and analyse the source speech enough; it is impossible to show the live process of notes being taken or how comprehension and time lag/*décalage* relate unless using impractical solutions (OHPs, black boards); students are too linear in their note-taking and do not work enough at the macro-level of the speech. Responses show that all the educators surveyed are interested in using the digital pen with their students; nearly all of them would recommend the tool to other trainers; the great majority of them think that using the pen could help them to be more efficient in their teaching and would provide them with a better diagnosis of their students' qualities and deficiencies. The great majority think that establishing a cross-fertilisation process in note-taking assessment in their classroom would benefit all students and that the digital pen would help peer-assessment and group work. Positive feedback was reported in relation to the Smartpen's ability to track the sequence of notes taken throughout a speech, to clearly show how *décalage* and comprehension are related, to locate examples of unclear notes, notes that are too copious for the content contained in the speech, as well as gaps where notes could or should have been made, usually due to lack of clarity of the source speech or in its comprehension. The main questions asked and the caveats put forward by the respondents are about the time to introduce the pen and install the equipment in their classroom; the time required to retrieve the data and send feedback to students; and the costs related to its purchase and use (pens, micro-dotted paper). But overall no one really doubts the relevance, usefulness and significance of the tool.

This data is invaluable insofar as educators from different backgrounds, of different ages, with different teaching experience, who are practising and teaching in different contexts, have expressed their view on the use of digital pen in the classroom, its advantages and disadvantages. Such feedback on the usability and relevance of the technology for consecutive interpreting training confirms the importance of the benefits of the use of digital pen technology in interpreter training.

As already mentioned, the technologisation of our world forces T&I practitioners to stay in tune with technological developments in their area of work (Drechsel 2013). I believe this applies and extends to T&I educators and trainers. As Lindquist showed in his study of simultaneous interpreting (2005), advances in technology have begun to help us to examine empirical data in different digital forms and offer trainers the possibility of making assumptions easy to apply practically in the classroom (see also Blasko Mayor & Amparo 2007; Hansen & Shlesinger 2007; Sandrelli 2012; Winteringham 2010). The example presented here illustrates how this can be conducted and will hopefully be beneficial to the profession in the long term.

5.2.2 Digital pen technology and a new hybrid mode of interpreting

The previous section is a good example of how technology introduced in the classroom as part of a sound pedagogical project can inform training and possibly practice. I will now discuss how the discovery of this technology proved also to be beneficial for research on interpreting modes, with promising applications in the profession.

Stemming from and elaborating on the conclusion about the use of the technology in the classroom, I later on decided to test the amenability of the digital pen if used in a hybrid mode of interpreting, in a consecutive interpreting context, where both consecutive and simultaneous modes are mixed. Because of the specific recording features of the digital pen, I became interested in research on this hybrid mode of interpreting using the new device.

Most interpreters tend to find consecutive interpreting assignments which require the understanding, memorisation and note-taking of a speech rather difficult and stressful. For this reason, performance enhancing technology is a resource welcome by interpreters, especially if technology is available to reduce the strain on short-term memory retention (the memory in action between the moment a speech is heard and notes representing it taken). Technology-assisted interpreting has long been of particular interest to trainers, practitioners and students seeking to find ways of integrating technological applications to assist them in their everyday professional life.

In 1999, for example, Michele Ferrari, a European Commission interpreter, was the first professional interpreter to employ digital technology by recording the source speech of a commissioner, then playing it back from his digital recording device, and interpreting it simultaneously. For the first time, a consecutive interpretation was performed simultaneously. In an interview, given in 2002, Ferrari justified his choice:

> I have always felt a sense of dissatisfaction in performing a consecutive, as if it was a constant struggle against impossible odds. Indeed, I firmly believe it is impossible to do a perfect consecutive, when faced with a difficult, dense and fast speech. Even

in the best consecutive of this world, there is always a little something missing. [...]
This [consecutive interpreting] entails a lack of rigour, which has always troubled
me ever since my first consecutive, and which led me to find a better solution, in
order to fully respect the speaker's original speech, in all its aspects. (Gomes, 2002,
p. 5).

This original approach to a 'digitally remastered' consecutive interpretation and this new mode triggered lots of interest from researchers and, from then on, several studies were conducted. As indicated in Hamidi and Pöchhacker (2007, p. 277–278), various practitioners have trialled different tools to test the efficiency of digital assistance when performing a long consecutive interpretation. For example, Ferrari carried out tests at the DG Interpretation with various devices in 2002 and 2003 (p. 277). These initial trials were soon followed respectively in 2003 and 2005 by those of John Lombardi and Erik Camayd-Frexas, two American interpreters who found the technique very useful for court interpreting assignments (Lombardi 2003, Camayd-Frexas 2005). In particular, Hamidi completed her Master's thesis on the subject in 2006, carried out a study and collected data on the hybrid simultaneous consecutive mode, also called 'SimConsec'. As reported by Pöchhaker (2012), other studies have been conducted since, especially by several masters' students: Sienkiewicz in 2010, Hawel in 2010, Richter in 2010, and Hiebl in 2011.

As most attempts have shown, and as expressed in Hamidi and Pöchhacker (2007), the new simultaneous consecutive mode allows an 'improvement in quality' (p.278) and 'is praised for its increased accuracy and completeness' (p.278). Because 'note-taking is no longer necessary [which] allows the interpreter to devote more attention to listening and comprehension' (p.278) it 'permitted enhanced interpreting performances' and was 'considered a viable technique' (p.288), despite some caveats about poor communication with the public. Indeed, even if the abovementioned studies have found an enhanced accuracy and completeness in the interpretations in the new mode, most have also pointed out a poorer audience contact and interaction during the simultaneous part of the task.

In 2012–2013, I decided to carry out a study to compare the interpreting performance of interpreters who used the conventional consecutive interpreting mode and this new hybridised mode with the aid of the digital pen. The main differences between this study and those previously undertaken lied in the equipment used (the interpreters could take notes with the pen), and in various criteria (the language pair, the experience of the interpreters, and the choice of variables: accuracy, eye contact, hesitation phenomena and speech flow).

Previous experiments and studies conducted to investigate the relevance and viability of the hybrid mode, labelled it or referred to it in different ways, e.g. as "Digitally remastered consecutive" or "Technology assisted consecutive" (Ferrari, 2002), "DRAC – Digital recorder assisted consecutive" (Lombardi, 2003), "Digital voice recorder assisted CI" (Camayd-Frexas, 2005), or "SimConsec" (Hamidi and Pöchhacker, 2007). I opted for the term *Consec-simul with notes* (or shortened as *Consec-simul*) to underline the fact that the interpreter still works with a pen and paper, and therefore that notes are still possible. This label also reflects the combination of both modes, consecutive and simultaneous, and the way the interpretation unfolds. The steps involved in consecutive interpreting are: listening, understanding, memorising and note-taking; and the steps involved in simultaneous interpreting are: listening, understanding and simultaneously expressing the content in the target language.

Using Gile's (1995a) now familiar Effort Models, by which Gile conceptualises the interpreting act as a series of efforts to be coordinated and managed to perform well, the operating processes undertaken in the *Consec-simul with notes* mode could be mapped as follows:

Phase 1:	Listening 1 and analysis 1
	Short-term memory operations
	Note-taking
Phase 2:	Listening 2 and analysis 2
	Short-term memory operations
	Long-term memory operations (reconstructing the speech)
	Note-reading/Retrieving information/Anticipation/
	Operating the pen
	Production

During phase 1, the effort components are identical to those for a traditional consecutive performance except that the interpreter knows that he/she will hear the speech a second time and interpret it simultaneously, and that he/she will have the possibility of slowing down or speeding up the audio playback with the digital pen. The interpreter is therefore likely to take notes in a different way and perhaps focus more on the structure of the speech, or write prompts about the pen features to use at a certain time during the interpretation. This 'anticipatory' knowledge is likely to lead to more economical note-taking, with a focus on the macro-linguistic and structural elements of the speech.

During phase 2, the effort components that are usually required and coordinated in simultaneous interpretation are facilitated by the fact the interpreter hears the content of the speech for the second time. This 'recently-acquired familiarity' with the content, coupled with specific notes the interpreter may have taken, should facilitate management of the extra load that the added coordination and management of operations may bring (e.g. anticipation, re-reading and matching notes from the first hearing, using other functions of the pen, such as slowing down or speeding up the playback).

The study

The study aimed at comparing interpreting performances delivered in two different modes, namely the "traditional" consecutive mode and the new dual hybrid mode, *Consec-simul with notes,* whereby the interpreter can perform from their notes as well as from playing back the recorded source speech. It specifically focussed on comparing the interpreting performance of four professional interpreters (working in the English-French pair) on the basis of accuracy, source-target correspondence and fluency.

The study also aimed at measuring the level of communication or interaction interpreters have with their audience when interpreting in one mode or the other. Participants were informed of this aim and were asked to consider the two other people in the room and the camera as their 'audience' during their interpretations. This is an important point to underline, since we wanted to see if these interpreters would attempt to improve the 'lack of eye contact' aspect previously mentioned. If so, this might suggest that if being told, or even trained, interpreters might be able to 'control' what appears as a drawback in the use of such technology, and be more natural and communicative.

The viability of the hybrid mode using the digital pen in the profession was also tested. The focus was therefore put on the interpreters' perspective about the use of the *Consec-simul with notes* mode with the Smartpen, in a real life situation, to determine if they would consider using the tool in their future practice. The full methodology, procedure and results can be found in an article published in 2014 (Orlando 2014) but are summed up hereafter.

Four French-English interpreters accepted to undertake the test and to interpret two speeches consecutively, one as a traditional consecutive interpretation, the other in the hybrid mode. The equipment used for the *Consec-simul with notes* performance was the digital pen Livescribe Smartpen, model Pulse™, and an A5 Livescribe notebook of micro-chipped paper. The experiment was conducted in the English-French pair and the analysis was made on the interpretations of speeches delivered in English and interpreted into French. The texts used for the study comprised speeches that were similar in terms of topic (transatlantic relations), length and density of information. Both speeches had been previously video-recorded from a delivery by the same English native speaker. The objectives of the study were explained to the participants as follows: "Our aim is to test the validity of the use of digital pen technology in the *Consec-simul with notes* mode compared to the conventional consecutive one. Previous comparative studies have shown better accuracy but a lack of eye contact in the hybrid mode of interpreting; therefore the experiment will also aim at checking the accuracy of the interpretation in both modes and also the eye contact instances with your audience". Before starting the actual experiment, the interpreters were given half an hour to get used to the pen functions, and were also given the opportunity to interpret in *Consec-simul* from another speech, of similar topic and length. Attention was paid in particular to the possibility to accelerate or to slow down the playback of the recording, should some passages of the source speech be too slow or too fast. Each video-recorded source speech in English was played without pause to the interpreter who then had to interpret it into French. Interpreters were allowed a 15-minute break between speeches. Interpretations were all video-recorded. After the experiment, participants were asked to stay in the room to fill in a questionnaire about their impressions and feelings.

After the experiment, the features of the interpreted performances (accuracy, eye contact instances, hesitation phenomena and duration and speed of speeches) were measured and analysed from the objective factors captured on the video. To measure the performance of the interpreters in terms of accuracy in each mode, each sentence of each speech was chunked in different 'units of meaning' (Seleskovitch, 1989), representing facts and ideas which were then aggregated. Each recorded interpretation was then transcribed orthographically (with the hesitations reported) and compared to the source speech, with the different units of meaning counted down, for each interpreter, in each mode of interpreting. The measurement consisted in checking the number of units of meaning understood by the interpreters and rendered fully in their performance. The way the rendition was phrased and its effect on an audience were not measured.

As an indication of how communicative each interpreter was in each mode, each eye contact instance with members of the audience was reported, according to the fact they were short or long, i.e. more or less than 1.5 second. Research in oculesics (the elements of kinesics dedicated to eye-related nonverbal communication) has shown that eye contact instances in a public-speaking situation indicate more or less interest, attention and involvement with the audience (Beebe 1974). Studies on gaze (length of gaze, frequency of glances, patterns of fixation) have indicated that speakers usually assign a more frequent and longer glance to the audience when they know their topic well, and that an increase in the length amount of eye contact generated by a speaker significantly increases the speaker's credibility (Gu and Badler 2006, Beebe 1974). During the interpreting performance, shorter eye contact occurrences seem to indicate simply the acknowledgement of the communication situation and the interpreter's awareness of an audience to connect with. Longer eye contact occurrences seem to indicate the interpreter is engaging more deeply with the recipients of the interpretation and is speaking directly to members of the audience.

The measurement of hesitation phenomena was done by counting the number of pauses, hesitations, false starts, etc, for each interpreter in each mode. Measuring these would indicate if there are more occurrences in one mode or another which would affect the fluency of the interpretation. "Disfluencies" as Garnham called them, such as 'hesitations, pauses, ums and ahs, corrections, false starts, repetitions, interjections, stuttering and slips of the tongue' (Garnham, 1985, p.206), have an impact on the fluency of the interpretation as they indicate hesitations in understanding the content, in retrieving the meaning of words or symbols noted down, in finding the right syntactical construction in the target production, but also nervous tension on the part of the interpreter. Goffman considers these 'linguistically detectable faults' or 'influencies' (1981, p.172) as manifestations of the efforts of reasoning and formulation which accompany linguistic production. As summarised by Mead (2000), the skill of professional speakers, such as the university lecturer or the radio announcer, is to control output in such a way as to hide these efforts and any hesitations they may entail. No 'production crisis' or 'backstage considerations' (p. 91), are allowed to betray moments of doubt or distraction. The speaker thus maintains control of any hesitations which could surface as 'linguistically detectable faults'. As Mead indicates (2000, p.91), 'Goffman's discussion provides an interesting theoretical basis for evaluation of fluency. Given that interpreters can to all intents and purposes be considered professional speakers, the definition of fluency by default (i.e. absence of influencies) can also prove relevant to evaluation of interpreting.'

Duration of target speeches and flow speed were a relevant element to measure as differences between both modes may be revealed at this level too. In comparing the two modes, we wanted to see if interpretations in the hybrid mode would be longer than the source speech, in particular if interpreters decided to use the slow-down feature of the play back the digital pen offers. Usually interpreters are trained in consecutive interpreting along the recommendation that the interpretation should be briefer than the original (Herbert, 1952, p.67–68), even if some leeway in the structure and content of the interpretation and/or some linguistic requirements may lengthen the production sometimes. In contrast, in simultaneous interpreting, the output generally follows more closely the source speech and the interpretation is expected to be as long as the original. In testing the viability of the new mode and the potentially better production in this mode, it was also pertinent to measure the duration and the word output in relation to the flow speed. To do so, each performance was timed and the total number of words was divided by the total duration of each speech. Interpreters who used the slow-down feature indicated it in the questionnaire they had to fill in.

Finally, to collect participants' perspective on the mode and the potential use of the technology in professional practice, a questionnaire was distributed at the end of the experiment. It consisted of nine open-ended questions and was presented to participants after their performance in the *Consec-simul* mode.

Results

The accuracy of interpretations was calculated based on units of meaning being conveyed in the interpretation. The collected data shows that when interpreting in the *Consec-simul* hybrid mode, the interpreters were more accurate and rendered more source information than in the conventional consecutive mode. This matched and confirmed what previous studies on technology-assisted consecutive interpreting had shown (Lombardi 2003, Vivas 2003, Camayd-Frexas 2005, Hamidi and Pöchhacker 2007, Hiebl 2011).

As already explained, the interpreters were told that in previous comparative studies, results had shown a lack of contact with the listeners in the technology assisted mode and that the study of their own interaction with the 'audience' would be one of the objectives of that test.

Depending on the mode of interpreting, the interaction between the interpreter and the audience differs. 'Simultaneous interpreting means tighter time constraints during production' (Mead, 2012, p.181) and may not provide enough room to naturally connect with the audience, whereas for an interpretation in the consecutive mode, the interpreter is the one who sets the pace during the production phase and can devote more attention to monitoring his/her output than in simultaneous as part of the Production Effort (Gile, 2001). Also, simultaneous interpreting is generally conveyed from a booth or in *chuchotage* and interpreters do not generally have to establish eye contact with the listeners. Consequently, one would naturally expect better interaction and more communication in the consecutive mode and indeed, as our data showed, more eye contact instances overall occurred in the traditional consecutive interpretations.

The data, however, showed that interpreters acknowledged the presence of their audience and interacted with their listeners also in the hybrid mode. Three interpreters out of four had more eye contact with the audience in the traditional mode, but one of them had actually more eye contact overall in the second speech than during the first.

What was interesting to note too was that the differential ratio 'long consistent eye contact/short eye contact instances' was lesser in the *Consec-simul* mode than in traditional consecutive. In contrast to what some of the earlier comparative studies revealed, there is little evidence here of a uniformly lower interaction in the hybrid mode. In fact, all interpreters maintained eye contact with the audience, with a steady number of long instances in the second speech (with one interpreter having twice as many instances of long eye contact with the audience in the second speech).

Considering the above-mentioned research in oculesics (Gu and Badler 2006, Beebe 1974), we can assume that the longer the eye contact, the more engaged interpreters are with the audience, the greater their assuredness in delivery and the deeper their command of the speech must be. If this communicative behaviour in the simultaneous part of the task is linked with the fact that they were alerted to the issue beforehand, this may indicate that with a certain degree of awareness, and even more importantly, with training, interpreters may be perfectly able to stay well connected with their audience and appear natural, even when providing the simultaneous interpretation. The fact that interpreters hear the speech for the second time when interpreting in this mode must also facilitate this capacity to communicate naturally.

In the study, the number of occurrences of hesitations (false starts, unfilled pauses, filled pauses with instances of "ers, ums, ahs", repetitions, redirections) was noted down and reported in the transcription of each individual performance in each mode. The data collected showed that 'disfluencies' are more frequent in the traditional consecutive than in the *Consec-simul* mode, and for all interpreters. This is not surprising as the effort required in consecutive interpreting to read notes, to retrieve meaning and logical structure of the ST, and to make a decision on the best reformulation, may often lead to more hesitations in the production phase than in the simultaneous mode where the interpreter follows the flow and pace of the speaker. Gile (1995) puts forward the argument that simultaneity [of listening and speaking] can sometimes make semantic and syntactic choices easier for the interpreter.

Based on the observations during the experiment and during the analysis of the video recorded data, and on Mead's aforementioned comments regarding evaluation of interpreting performances (see above), fewer disfluencies are unsurprisingly indicative of better fluency in the delivery/production. This is an important point in the comparison of the two modes because, as Mead (2000, p.90) also points out, 'surveys among interpreters and conference participants confirm the importance of fluency as a determinant of quality in interpreting'. And quoting Altman (1994) he also indicates that 'fluency […] is the one single aspect of an interpretation which most palpably distinguishes a professional performance from that of a trainee'.

When linked with the data concerning accuracy and the different ratio of instances of long/short eye contact in the hybrid mode, the above-mentioned ideas seem to suggest that during an interpretation in the *Consec-simul with notes* mode a higher level of accuracy (comprehension and rendition of the source text) may co-occur with greater fluency (less disfluencies) of the delivery and superior communication with the public (more consistent eye contact instances). And this may allow a professional performance and service of a better quality. Should this be backed up by further studies on a larger scale, the impact of the use of digital pen technology on interpreting pedagogy and training could be of wide-ranging importance.

One of the objectives of the test was also to check if the length and speed of interpretations would change depending on the mode of interpreting opted for. The general immediately visible conclusion drawn from the data was that interpretations were nearly all of the same length as the source text and delivered in a narrow range of speed (109wpm to 126wpm). There was therefore no real blatant difference in the duration of interpretations in each mode. Three consecutive interpretations were slightly shorter than the original, as could be expected. All interpretations in the hybrid mode were approximately the same length as the original, even when the interpreters used the slow-down feature of the pen. It seems reasonable to say that, should interpreters decide to work in *Consec-simul with notes*, they are likely to provide an interpretation of approximately the same length as the original speech, and not much longer, as might be feared by some.

The interpreters in this sample all declared that they felt more confident in the *Consec-simul with notes* mode, that they provided a better performance, and that they preferred interpreting in this mode. All also added they would use it in future professional settings, provided they engage in or invest in more (self-) directed training with the digital pen and its features. All participants indicated that they took fewer or different notes when interpreting in the hybrid mode. Investigations on the note-taking conventions of interpreters when working in this mode should be encouraged as they would certainly open new doors for both interpreting training and practice.

It is important to note that the number of participants tested in this study was small and the small size disallowed any claim that their experiences and attitudes were representative of most interpreters. However, the results of this study were promising insofar as the use of digital pen technology in the hybrid mode of interpreting *Consec-simul with notes* seemed to indicate a better quality of performances and a better comfort in performing. Further research should be encouraged to gather more evidence of this and to motivate training programmes to introduce the technology in their curricula, with the aim of both facilitating the work of interpreters and improving the service to end-users who expect high quality in the performances of professionals.

Being an active conference interpreter myself and working either in consecutive or simultaneous modes, I can see here a lot of potential applications when simultaneous cannot be provided from a booth (for contextual, technical or financial reasons) and interpretation in the consecutive mode is required. When working in a consecutive context, it is always hard to anticipate whether the speaker will take the floor to ask a two-minute question or deliver a fifteen-minute speech. Using the digital pen while the speaker takes the floor gives interpreters the opportunity to take notes as usual and not use the recording if the intervention is short, or to play back the audio if it is a longer, more difficult passage, and deliver a simultaneous interpretation. The tool used in the hybrid mode could also be particularly useful in settings where the provision of equipment is limited (conflict zones, disaster zones), in court interpreting where accuracy is paramount, in mental health consultations where the clinician needs the full interpretation of what the patient is saying, and more generally in any context where long consecutive interpretation is required.

A word on training in the hybrid mode

The hybrid mode of interpreting described above seems to offer various intriguing possibilities for the profession but, as for any mode to be acquired, training activities should be developed to maximise these advantages. Given the feedback received from the participants in the study, and the necessity to train interpreters in how to operate the pen if they wanted to use it in such a mode, we decided to develop and implement a few training activities in the course of the master degree curriculum at Monash University.

In the hybrid *Consec-simul* mode, the advantage is that the interpreter already knows the content of the speech when (s)he starts interpreting, can use the notes (s)he has taken in anticipation or backup, and can also slow down the playback if necessary. Even if the simultaneous interpretation is facilitated, the difficulty of working in this mode lies in the various tasks to be completed simultaneously: starting the playback, listening and understanding, speaking, reading the notes, and operating the pen if necessary. That is why performing in this unorthodox mode requires specific training.

Our interpreting students are trained in consecutive interpreting (long and short) from the early beginning of their masters' course. Simultaneous interpreting is introduced little by little in the second semester only and then fully for the rest of their training. As explained in 5.2.1, they are introduced to the Smartpen for their note-taking exercises in second semester. This is also when they are exposed to some cognitive activities to prepare them to simultaneous interpreting, and especially to listen and speak at the same time. That is why it was decided to start working in the hybrid mode in the second half of that semester, when students know how to use the pen and have already experienced split attention exercises. The activities implemented were calqued on the training in consecutive or in simultaneous: easy speeches to start with (personal narratives, speeches with logical arguments, etc.), which were delivered at an easy pace while students took notes with the digital pen which was recording the speech. Then, they were taught to trigger the speech playback, to use the ear set and start interpreting simultaneously.

Research would be needed to determine what moment would be best to start training in this mode, but it appeared convenient to start 'between' consecutive and simultaneous, seeing the hybrid mode maybe as a step towards simultaneous interpreting. As we started training in *Consec-simul* recently only, we do not have much distance yet to comment on the experiment and it is difficult to see what works or not, but future developments and projects will help determine sound pedagogical strategies. The fact is that beyond the 'technical' steps used in operating the pen, there was apparently nothing very different between learning to work in this mode or the two others. And even after just a few weeks of work in *Consec-simul*, students were enthusiastic in adopting the mode. This is already a very encouraging sign which might lead to the future adoption of a new mode of interpreting in training institutions.

5.2.3 Developments in training, research and in the profession

Since 2010 and the appearance of digital pen technology in the interpreting classroom and the interpreting profession, the word has spread that its use for consecutive interpreting training and practice is a definite possibility. I presented the technology for the first time at the University of Trieste conference on innovation in interpreting research in June 2010. Because of the innovative dimension of this discovery and of the uniqueness of the new approach to consecutive interpreting training, I was invited to present the tool at the European Commission DG Interpretation in Brussels during their DG Interpretation-Universities conference in March 2011. The digital pen and the pedagogical sequences applied to consecutive interpreting were showcased then and attracted a great deal of interest from trainers and researchers. The DG Interpretation has even considered using the tool in intake tests to assess candidates' note-taking skills, and also asked their staff going on missions where consecutive interpreting would be required to envisage interpreting in the hybrid mode of interpreting using the digital pen.

This technology and its potential merits has now been around for about 5 years, and when one tries to locate academic publications or instances of its practical use, several interesting examples show up. Online searches for example reveal that several university students have used the digital pen technology applied to interpreting as their thesis topic (e.g. Hiebl 2011; Kostal 2011; Estébanez

2012). The technology is also referred to in several articles and book chapters dealing with the application of new technology in interpreter training and research (e.g. Cardoen 2012; Kellett Bidoli 2012; Sandrelli 2012). Also, various institutions have implemented the use of the tool in their training programmes (e.g. KU Leuven in Belgium, Mainz/Germersheim in Germany, Heriot Watt in the UK, The Monterey Institute in the USA).

In the professional field, several practitioners report of their using this technology or others in their practice (Orlando, 2015a). On the blog *Endless Possibilities Talks*, for example, one can follow among other things a videorecorded session on "Technology options for interpreting" (Endless Possibilities Talks 2012) where various practitioners from different countries (e.g., UK, USA, Germany and Spain) share ideas and explain how they use digital technology to perform 'a better job when interpreting' and to also 'reduce costs and incidental elements'. In particular, Esther Navarro-Hall, a US-based conference and court interpreter and instructor at the Monterey Institute of International Studies, and Martin Esposito, a conference interpreter based in the UK and Italy, focus on the use of the *Livescribe Smartpen*, which they are both using in their practice. They show its numerous advantages and benefits during practical assignments, in comparison to more traditional digital recorders or Mp3 players. Navarro-Hall also organises workshops on the hybrid *SimConsec* mode in the USA, where trainees are introduced to 'an exciting combination of two interpreting skills + portable technology, which is quickly becoming the technique of choice for today's interpreter' (Navarro-Hall 2012). On another blog, *Interpreting.info*, practitioners' questions about this new mode and digital tools are discussed, and even if some doubts are expressed by some, others clearly point out that those in the profession who are not aware of digital devices like the Smartpen somehow 'choose to be left behind' (Interpreting.info 2012). Another interesting online initiative for interpreters to share ideas is the *#IntJC*, the Interpreting Journal Club, led from Japan by professional interpreter Lionel Dersot, which organises Tweetchats, a free web-based service. One of the Club's sessions was dedicated to "Digital Pen and Note-taking" (*#IntJC* the Interpreting Journal Club 2012). The script of the session, available online in their archive section, clearly shows interest in the use of the

Smartpen from researchers and trainers like Heidi Salaets from KU Leuven, Belgium, who reports using the Smartpen for research and training purposes, or also Barry Olsen from the Monterey Institute of International Studies, as well as from different practitioners who already use the pen during missions or plan to.

On these various fora, many different conclusions and opinions are expressed by users but the fact remains that, whether they are positive or negative, digital technology cannot be ignored. Alexander Drechsel, a European Commission interpreter who has been writing for some time on the relation between interpreters and technology, recently concluded one of his web-based articles with these words: 'Interpreters today stand right in the middle of a 'tsunami' of technological and social change. We must act and 'understand the wave' to be able to ride it and not drown' (Drechsel 2013). To be able to understand and master the wave, I strongly believe – as I have discussed throughout this book – that synergies between all stakeholders must be promoted and that practitioners, researchers and trainers need to collaborate to identify and recommend what works, what does not, or what requires particular training.

Several studies in Interpreting Studies have shown that previous technological developments and innovations in interpreting practice (e.g. telephone interpreting, video-link interpreting) have resulted in qualitatively different protocols and have offered new practical opportunities (Braun 2011; Moser-Mercer 2005; Napier 2011; Ozolins 2011). This example presented the use of a new technology, new possibilities in training, a new facet and a new mode of interpreting applied to new contexts, and the way they can be implemented in a 21st century training programme. The pivotal role of training has been underlined, especially when looking at it from a practice-informed angle and a process going from 'practice to theory and back in interpreting' (Setton, 2010). Following the suggestions made earlier on the role of T&I research in training, this case study also illustrates how academic knowledge, technological awareness and professional experience can turn mere intuitions into innovative outputs to be considered in training, with an invaluable impact on the profession in the future.

5.3 Translation process and product-oriented evaluation

The third example chosen to illustrate how professional experience and a good knowledge of the industry in which T&I practitioners work can be turned into pedagogical tools along academic lines will focus on an innovative approach in evaluating translations when training future practitioners. The focus is on the introduction at master's level of translation evaluation tools which combined product-oriented evaluation criteria used in the professional world by agencies, international organisations and the Australian national accreditation authority with process-oriented and didactic elements which help translator trainees to adopt a self-reflexive method of work.

Having worked as a professional translator for many years and in different regions, I have often been assessed by clients and agencies who used sometimes very different assessment strategies and tools (revisers commenting on your work, managers using different types of grids to evaluate samples of your work on a monthly basis and to monitor the quality of your work, etc.). When I started training future translators, I decided it would be relevant to bring some of these realities and instruments in their training and make them aware of those professional practices. As already discussed in section 3.3.3.2, I believe a translator training curriculum, based on both academic and vocational content, should focus on translation both as a product and as a process, and should envisage assessing students in a formative and summative manner. At the same time, it should also include evaluation rubrics and criteria and revision parameters used in the industry and the professional world (normative evaluation).

The following evaluation approach is based on two complementary marking grids that I designed when I started teaching in the Master of Interpreting and Translation Studies at Monash University, and which are based on both didactic and formative elements as well as evaluation criteria (e.g. textual and extra-textual or objective and subjective factors) used by agencies, institutions, and international organisations in the workplace.

The approach
Trainees in Translation Studies postgraduate courses (at least in Australia but I assume it is also the case in other regions) generally join such programmes from

different universities and backgrounds, and even different countries. Very often, they do not know much about the methods of evaluation used in the T&I industry, about the numerous tasks beyond the linguistic transfer practitioners have to complete, or about the methodology requirements which allow translators to understand the translational process and identify their own weaknesses and strengths. However, during their training, they will have to be made aware of the professional practices and tools used by agencies and organisations worldwide, and learn best practices and methods to become efficient practitioners. This, I believe, can be done consistently if different types of activities and evaluations are implemented in the course, mirroring the sector's practices and norms, as well as the different learning stages, and if the evaluations follow appropriately the stages of the training. Such tools have been introduced at Monash University. Because the classes are taught by practitioners, academics and professionals, and because the curriculum is based on a balance of academic and professional activities, students are assessed throughout their training both in a formative way (assessment relevant to the training stage) and a normative way (assessment taking into account norms of the sector). Whether the student's translation is assessed in a product-oriented way (entry test, practical test, final exam, accreditation exam, *practicum* work, etc.) or in a process-oriented way (assessed tasks with different objectives at different stages of the training, formative exercises), instructors need different tools which give them the possibility to understand the strengths and weaknesses of the trainees' translation competence, and help them to choose appropriate remedial teaching strategies.

As I discussed in the first part of this book, today's and tomorrow's professionals must be aware of their profession requirements and specificities both at a local and a global level. Translators, in particular, can be offered jobs by clients who live out of their geographical region. Indeed, many global translation companies operate on a 24/7 basis and thus need translation platforms in different parts of the world. When these platforms (generally managed by local project managers) require translations, they contact translators in their time zone, even if the translation is commissioned from another region. Platforms based in Europe will send their translations to Europe-based translators, whereas platforms based in South America or in Asia will offer work to professionals based in these regions. The South Pacific region-based translators (e.g. in Australia, New Zealand) can therefore be asked to translate documents for a client based in Europe simply because of this geostrategic commercial arrangement and because their European counterparts are asleep when they are up. Training of future translators should therefore recognise these new realities and modalities of work and ensure that students become efficient professionals in a local *and* a global market, and are aware of the requirements and the norms of evaluation required in the T&I industry both locally and globally. In addition, training would aim to raise awareness of the different roles and functions required from translators in this field. Bearing in mind that students need to be well-prepared and well-equipped for the local and the global T&I market, and that they also need to be active participants in their learning process, different activities and evaluation tools can be implemented in the curriculum. In our programme, two main tools have been introduced in a student-centred approach. The first one includes different evaluation grids that combine didactic elements used in other fields of assessment as well as elements used by T&I agencies, by organisations worldwide, and by the Australian National Accreditation Authority for Translators and Interpreters (NAATI). The other major tool is a translator's diary, based on different drafts of the translation and on the revision steps, which helps students to justify their strategy or to refer to research. These evaluation tools aim to make future translators aware of the role of the translator as a thinking professional, of their own practice, of theoretical approaches relevant to their practice, but also of the normative demands of the T&I industry.

As clearly discussed by Martinez Melis and Hurtado Albir (2001, p. 273–274), translation evaluation has long been a very subjective exercise. However, they show that in recent decades the academic world has seen the gradual introduction of objective criteria into translation evaluation, that analytical models of translation evaluations have been designed, and that the progress seen in Translation Studies has led to a better understanding of the translational process and of its evaluation.

When dealing with translation assessment, the first step is to define what a translation is. In light of Larose's view (1998, p. 6) the term stands either for a transformation process of a source text (ST) into a target text (TT), or for the result of this transformation, it is crucial to make a clear distinction between the process and the product. Another important element to consider is the fact that many translation trainees come from language programmes where they had to perform translation exercises, mainly with purely linguistic objectives, and have therefore acquired certain habits and expectations in relation to assessment. As Schäffner explains (1997a, p. 4), a common practice in assessing translations in language acquisition courses is to count linguistic errors and deduct points for each error and add bonus points for good choices and solutions. In a programme aiming at training future professionals along theoretical and practical lines, students and instructors must all understand that a translation is not a simple exercise in vocabulary, grammar and syntax tested against a model translation; that the assessment of a translation cannot be limited to a linguistic approach; that there is not just one way to evaluate translations; that the evaluation objectives and criteria may differ from one assignment to another; and that a translation is always evaluated according to certain expectations (e.g. textual for the author and the reader, extra-textual for the agency, the client or the commissioner, both textual and extra-textual for an instructor, etc.). Students must be sensitised to this variety of expectations and situations.

As is often pointed out (see for example Gile 2005, Kelly 2005), the evaluation of translations is often considered a difficult exercise mainly because of the unstable nature of several of its elements, such as the objectives, the criteria, the methodology, or even the assessor. To implement a system which minimises such instability, the evaluation designer must carefully identify and define the nature of these elements. The methodology of the evaluation is one such unstable element which complicates the task of the assessor and must be thoroughly reflected upon when designing evaluation tools. Does the assessor compare the ST and the TT? How? Are the factors used objective or subjective? How are the difference marked and the factors weighted? If, for example, the view of Gouadec (1989, p. 53–54), that any translation error may be evaluated in terms of the damage it is likely to cause, is applied to a specific task, how are the errors weighted? Does any scale – that the student is aware of – exist for these elements at the time of the evaluation? Does the student have an opportunity to justify his or her choices and strategy?

In our programme, as in many others globally, the teaching team is also a variable element. Because the classes are taught both by academics and professionals, a high number of staff members are employed as 'sessionals' or on short term contracts. The resulting turnover increases the instability of our evaluation approach. New personnel need to be trained to use the specific tools employed in the programme. Moreover, the higher the number of language pairs, the greater the variation. If one also considers that the background, or the field and specialty of the assessor have an impact on the evaluation, then all these combined elements complicate any evaluation approach and system.

However daunting such variability may be, stable elements also exist in the translational process. The first one is the existence of a function for every translation. Training students to always clearly identify or define this function, the *skopos*, helps them to make appropriate decisions and choices (see Nord 1997, Schäffner 1997b). The second stable element is somehow related to the effect of the transfer in the TT. Unless specified otherwise in the translation brief provided by the client of the translation, every translated text, as an independent new text in the target culture, must bear an impeccable syntactic and linguistic quality. As Gile (2005, p. 14) points out, students must realise that beyond their proficiency in the ST language, and their ability to transfer a text into another language, they must always pay special attention to the quality of their writing in the language of the TT. These ideas were also put forward by Hönig (1995) who stresses that the decisive qualification of translators is not their knowledge of a foreign language and their subject-specific knowledge, but it is their knowledge of what texts are used for, and how they achieve their effects. These elements – function, effect and quality – should therefore be considered when designing evaluation tools.

In order to design an evaluation system and relevant assessment tools which would allow instructors to assess their students in relation to the above theoretical and methodological elements and a more professional, industry-based approach, we carried out a collection and analysis of different grids used in the translation sector by various agencies, organisations, and government departments that have quality assessment services. The fact that practitioners teach in the programme facilitated this collection, as grids are sent to them regularly by employers as assessment of their personal professional work. Unsurprisingly, the conclusion was that the majority of assessment services worldwide assess translations as products only, according to a balance of objective and subjective textual factors. Because of the vocational aspect of our training, we decided to design an evaluation grid which would be a reflection of what is used in the translation sector worldwide and would evaluate the translated text as a product. Elements such as function, quality, effect, appropriateness for the target audience, as well as respect of the brief of the translation, genre, and style would be assessed along with more objective textual factors, such as comprehension of the ST, accuracy in the transfer, linguistic quality, etc. However, because of the academic, student and research-centred nature of our training, we were not satisfied with a product-oriented grid only. In the course of their training students gain a foundation in theories of translation/interpreting and receive training in methods of research in Translation Studies. Upon completion, they are able to conceptualise Translation Studies as an academic discipline in its historical, cross-disciplinary and intercultural contexts. It was therefore relevant to design a second evaluation grid to assess the translated text in relation to the students' academic knowledge and the process of the translation, and taking into account extra-textual factors.

As I mentioned earlier, I believe that the role of any teacher is to disappear gradually and let each trainee become more and more independent and active in their learning process. As far as translation evaluation is concerned, this implies that whatever the task to be assessed is, students/trainees will get involved in the process and should always know what the objectives, criteria and methodology of the evaluations are. They should always be given as much information as possible about the tools used and the expectations and outcomes of any exercise or task.

Two distinct assessment grids were designed to be used according to the type of translation to be done and the type of evaluation to be carried out. The grids are complementary. They have been made up from a combination of elements used in the T&I sector, didactic elements, and NAATI criteria and requirements. Because of the student-centred approach of the course, the students are familiar with the grids and always know whether their work will be assessed in a process or a product oriented manner. As our course has been approved by NAATI, and as students who complete it successfully can be recommended for accreditation as professional translators without sitting the official external test, some evaluation criteria specific to NAATI had to be followed when we elaborated these grids. The NAATI evaluation system for translation tests is product-oriented and based on scales of mark deductions. Errors made by candidates are judged as minor, significant or serious, and in each category a certain number of points is deducted for a certain type of error. Factors considered for evaluation are objective and subjective textual factors (spelling, punctuation, grammar, word choice, insertion, omission, retention, etc.) and are graded depending on their effect on accuracy, reliability, meaning and the level of distortion to the overall meaning. Both grids are composed of three distinct parts. Different elements of the translated text are examined and marked. Both grids mark the translation out of 100, but with a different breakdown according to the type of evaluation. The marking rationale is that points are not deducted but granted. The *translation exercise* part is used to assess and give feedback on objective textual elements of the translated text. The *overall translation effect* part focuses on more subjective textual elements related to the effect produced by the translated text. The third part is what differentiates the two grids the most in terms of approach and objectives.

Grid A: For a product-oriented evaluation

This grid is used to assess the translation mainly on a textual and function/effect basis without considering the translational process and extra-textual elements. It can be used for any practice or final exam, accreditation test, professional competitive exam, or even in the industry.

TRANSLATION EXERCISE	/60
• Overall Comprehension of Source Text (misinterpretations with more or less effect on accuracy) 0 2 4 6 8 10 12	
• Overall Translation Accuracy / Transfer ST>TT (mistranslations with more or less effect on accuracy) 0 2 4 6 8 10 12	
• Omissions / Insertions (with more or less effect on accuracy) 0 2 4 6 8 • Terminology / Word Choices (affecting more or less the localised meaning) 0 2 4 6 8 • Grammatical Choices / Syntactic Choices (producing more or less distortion to the meaning) 0 2 4 6 8	
• Spelling Errors 0 2 4 6 • Punctuation Errors 0 1 2 3 • Formatting Errors 0 1 2 3	
OVERALL TRANSLATION EFFECT	/30
• Appropriateness for Target Audience 0 2 4 6 8 10 • Readability / Idiomatic Correctness 0 2 4 6 8 10	
Adherence to Brief: • Function / Completeness 0 1 2 4 6 • Style / Presentation / Genre 0 1 2 4	
ETHICAL and CONCEPTUAL QUESTIONS	/10
Question 1 0 1 2 3 4 5 Question 2 0 1 2 3 4 5	
OVERALL COMMENT: FINAL MARK:	/100

Ethics of the profession have an important place in our curriculum, so this element was incorporated in the third part of the grid along with some conceptual questions. During their test or exam, students have to perform a translation but also to answer ethical and conceptual questions. The ethical questions asked are generally realistic professional dilemmas that translators could face. Students are therefore asked to analyse the problem and provide a possible solution, but also to relate it to the AUSIT Code of Ethics used in Australia. The theoretical or conceptual questions asked require answers from students which must be linked to the theories to which they have been exposed in the course of the semester.

Grid B: For a process-oriented evaluation
With this evaluation grid, the focus is also on the inherent different stages of the translational process. The grid allows the assessor to evaluate the translation on

the same textual elements as Grid A, but in the third part the strategy, the methodology, the use of material and research, and the revision process applied by the student are also considered. Instructors will refer to the student's ITD (see below) to assess these different elements.

TRANSLATION EXERCISE		/50
• Overall Comprehension of Source Text (misinterpretations with more or less effect on accuracy)	0 2 4 6 8 10	
• Overall Translation Accuracy / Transfer ST>TT (mistranslations with more or less effect on accuracy)	0 2 4 6 8 10	
• Omissions / Insertions (with more or less effect on accuracy)	0 2 4 6 8	
• Terminology / Word Choices (affecting more or less the localised meaning)	0 2 4 6	
• Grammatical Choices / Syntactic Choices (producing more or less distortion to the meaning)	0 2 4 6	
• Spelling Errors	0 2 4 6	
• Punctuation Errors	0 1 2	
• Formatting Errors	0 1 2	
OVERALL TRANSLATION EFFECT		/20
• Appropriateness for Target Audience	0 2 4 6 8	
• Readability / Idiomatic Correctness	0 2 4 6 8	
Adherence to Brief:		
• Function / Completeness	0 1 2	
• Style / Presentation / Genre	0 1 2	
TRANSLATOR'S STRATEGY		/30
INTEGRATED TRANSLATOR'S DIARY (Reporting of problems, actions, decisions)		
• Use of material / Research	0 2 4 6 8 10	
• Strategy / Justifications / Report (Relevance of choices)	0 2 4 6 8 10	
• Revision / Proofreading	0 2 4 6 8 10	
OVERALL COMMENT:	**FINAL MARK:**	/100

To allow assessment of the translator's strategy and the extra-textual elements, students are asked to hand in their translation with an integrated translator's diary (ITD). The idea to ask students to write a translator's diary and to integrate it into their translation assignment comes from my personal experience as a translator and from different testimonies of professional translators who work in the programme. Experience shows that, in the 'real' translation world, it is crucial that translators keep a record of choices made and research undertaken. Indeed, they could be asked for justifications, sometimes months after the completion of the translation and, without any record of the research done at the time to decide for one translation or another, they may be incapable of explaining their choice. It is thus essential to make future professionals aware of the need to keep a diary for most of the translations that they undertake.

The didactic rationale for this diary stems directly from Gile's use of IPDR (the Integrated Problem and Decision Reporting) as a translator training tool, and also from our considerations regarding the necessity to implement metacognitive strategies in the students' training. Gile (2004, p. 1) states that 'two important factors to achieve high efficiency in the translation classroom are awareness by trainees of what they are doing when they translate, and awareness by instructors of what trainees are doing, as opposed to awareness of the characteristics of the product'.

The ITD is a report of the student's strategies for one assignment. With any text to be translated, translators are almost always caught in the 'literality vs. adaptation dilemma' – the translation should be as literal as possible but as free as necessary; or they have to do their translation following a specific brief imposed by the commissioner of the translation; or, because of the text's cultural or stylistic specificities or function, they have to carry out deep and specialised research and make very specific decisions. Therefore, they resort to different translation strategies within the same text. If, for example, a student decides to omit or insert a phrase or an idea for a reason that is justified to him or her, the omission or insertion may not be the error or inaccurate transfer the assessor thinks it is. It may be perfectly justified. One way to know if the strategies chosen by the future translators are relevant is to give them an opportunity to justify their choice.

The ITD helps students to realise that translation is far from automatic and that different phases, other than purely linguistic ones, are involved in the process (deep textual analysis, research, cultural awareness, proofreading, revising, etc.). Based on the drafts of the translation produced during the process, the ITD details the different problems encountered and presents the solutions found and the decisions made. The drafts are attached to the ITD, and the changes, made from one draft to the other with the Word 'comments' function, are commented on by the student and can easily be followed and reviewed by the assessor. In the diary, students are asked to provide information about the research they have carried out, the parallel texts they have found and their relevance, their approach and strategy to perform the translation, etc. They can also reflect on Translation Studies theories and explain whether they helped them to make choices. From one draft to the other, they also have the opportunity to show how they have thoroughly proofread or revised their translation. Undoubtedly, the ITD gives them the opportunity to reflect upon the process of translation, to justify and explain their strategy and their choices, and to comply better with the concepts they have been taught. It offers them the opportunity to show that they have explored different possibilities in the translation of a given passage. One very positive aspect of feedback from students is that they come to understand better, with this formative approach, why they have to learn theories and how theories can help them in the translational process.

The ITD is a tool which enables instructors to know their students better and to find adequate teaching and remedial strategies. It also gives the opportunity to conduct interactive and lively correction sessions, where, as suggested by Lörscher (1992, p. 160), the instructor and students can compare what they consider to be success in their own respective translations. As it is clearly recommended by Gile in relation to the IPDR (2004, p. 4), our ITD is a three phase pedagogical tool too. First, the students write and hand in their ITD with their translation. Second, the instructor reads, analyses and sums up the ITDs. Third, the instructor presents the summary to the class and opens the discussion. Needless to say, the pedagogical effectiveness of the ITD depends on the implementation of all the phases, even if it tends to increase the workload of students and instructors.

To ensure a good understanding of the principles and teaching philosophy underlying the approach presented here, the grids, the ITD, and the rationale for their implementation, are explained to the students at the beginning of their training. A special session on evaluation is held at the beginning of each semester during which the grids and ITD are presented and the different evaluation approaches (normative, summative and formative) are explained and discussed. The focus is put on the complementary nature of the tools. Students, but also staff members, who have been accustomed to different modes of evaluation are generally doubtful at best, and resistant at worst, to this new system which takes into account elements other than merely language transfer. Students often complain about the amount of work the ITD represents. It is generally only after the assessment of one or two tasks in such a process-oriented way that they recognise the value of the system. To ensure consistency in the evaluation of all the students in the course (about 60 students and up to 12 languages) and to limit the impact of the considerable turnover of staff members, as well as the resistance of some among them, new instructors are invited to attend the students' session on evaluation. To facilitate their use of the different assessment tools, descriptors to which they can resort to when using the grids have also been designed. Moreover, to maintain openness and flexibility in the approach, staff meetings are organised each semester to consider and discuss these instruments.

These different tools (the grids, the diary and also grid descriptors provided as a marking assistance tool) have allowed interesting developments in the programme as far as *training of the trainers* is concerned (as mentioned in 2.3 and 4.1). Whether academics teaching language classes and more used to undergraduate evaluation habits, or professionals lacking pedagogical and theoretical references, all instructors are asked to attend the induction session on assessment strategies, and all over the years have reported of the benefits of such an approach. As a consequence, I would say that beyond its pedagogical advantages, this approach to quality assessment and translation evaluation has also been a positive way to organise staff induction meetings, to train the trainers and to foster a collegial team spirit in the programme.

This case study is another example of the way professional practice and knowledge can be turned into pedagogical elements and into research on education as well. As explained, these professional rubrics were inspired by some used in agencies or institutions I have worked for as a professional translator, and others are used by NAATI, the Australian accreditation authority which approved our course, and relate therefore to the elements discussed earlier and the need to use material which reflects professional practice in training (Drugan 2013; Gouadec 2007; Quah 2006; Way 2008). As part of the metacognitive and formative approach underpinning the evaluation strategy, a translator diary has been introduced in the assessment process and enables students to discuss and justify their translation choices and strategy (Gile 2004). The diary allows students to combine practical and theoretical perspectives, and in this respect can be related to Pym's minimalist theory (discussed in 2.2). The idea that trainees need to be assessed in both a formative way (the way they reflect on the translation process), and a normative way (their product against professional norms used locally or globally) proved to be an original and successful approach, keeping a foot on each side of the divide.

The value of these tools in the training of future professional translators lies in the fact they have been created from a combination of theoretical, professional and pedagogical elements. In addition, the success in using them depends to a large extent on the way they are presented to trainees at the initial stage of their training and the way trainees are included in the learning process. If enough time is spent convincing them that the main objective of the approach is to ensure that they will acquire a good knowledge of their discipline, effective methods, and the ability to work autonomously in both local and global contexts, then they will adhere to the approach and become the efficient professionals we expect them to be. This is therefore an example of how practical experience and research can inform training and practice. It also shows how shared professional practice among teaching staff can lead to the development of new pedagogical material, to trainer training, and to awareness of contemporary practices for trainees.

Various articles and volumes dealing with the question of translation evaluation and quality assessment refer to these instruments (Drugan 2013; Gambier & Doorslaer 2012; Pokorn & Koskinen 2013; Şahin 2014; Washbourne 2014). Through these references, I have been able to measure that the approach has been of interest to others. Apparently the tools have either been introduced in other programmes or used for research purposes (Şahin 2014). This, to me, is evidence of the relevance and benefits of the new knowledge created by a view which aimed at blending elements from the two sides of the research/practice gap through pedagogy.

6 Conclusion

Some underlying assumptions of this book are that future professionals should become aware, during their training, of the need to be linguistically and theoretically well-equipped before starting practising, and should be enabled to reflect upon their practice autonomously. They also need extensive knowledge of their profession and industry, as well as a well-developed social and cultural awareness of the country/ies and markets in which they will work. It is through the correlation, combination and interaction of academic, empirical and contextual studies taught by academics, professionals and specialists that students will become well-trained and efficient translators and interpreters, adapted to the needs and demands of their industry.

The aim of this book was to show how the pedagogical, theoretical and professional dimensions of the T&I field need to be considered as part of a whole in the training of professional translators and interpreters. As I discussed, my own professional experience has enabled me to realise that the interaction between these dimensions is an asset that should be exploited. I have little doubt that practice informs research, research informs practice, and findings from both worlds inform training and education in a cyclical manner. However, the links between these different aspects of the field are still not always clearly established and the academic/vocational dichotomy still prevails. Many practitioners doubt the usefulness of research, or are critical of the prevalence of theory in courses with no obvious applicability to practice, despite the fact that many researchers in the field are or were at one time practitioners. One important factor is that the academic realm does not facilitate the integration of personal, practical, and professional observations into its research and theoretical approaches.

As I have suggested in these pages, this situation could change if more practitioners wrote about their practice and were given opportunities to be involved in research projects and to turn their experience into academic material that could be of use in the training and education of future professionals. The examples presented are examples of practical observations and questions that have been turned into academic reflections and publications and then applied to training with the aim of feeding them back into practice. They illustrate how practice and research can inform each other, and how knowledge gained from these interactions can be turned into pedagogical tools to be used in T&I training and education. I hope this contribution will convince readers of the pivotal role of training in the quest to cross the divide between the two sides of the fence and to underline the important role *practisearchers* could play.

Reference list

Alexieva, B 1994, 'On teaching note-taking in consecutive interpreting', in C Dollerup & A Lindegaard (eds.), *Teaching Translation and Interpreting 2*, John Benjamins, Amsterdam/Philadelphia, pp. 199–206.

Al-Qinai, J 2000, 'Translation quality assessment; strategies, parameters and procedures', *Meta*, vol. 45, no. 3, pp. 497–519.

Andres, D 2002, *Konsekutivdolmetschen und Notation*, Peter Lang, Frankfurt.

Andres, D, & Behr M (eds.) 2015, *To Know How to Suggest... Approaches to Teaching Conference Interpreting*, Frank & Timme, Berlin.

Arumí, M & Esteve, O 2006, 'Using instruments aimed at self-regulation in the consecutive interpreting classroom: Two case studies', *Electronic Journal of Foreign Language Teaching*, vol .3, no. 2, pp. 158–189.

Australian Electoral Commission 2010, 'Translated information and telephone interpreter service', viewed 30 July 2010, http://www.aec.gov.au/About_AEC/Translated_information/

Barrett, E 2007, 'Foucault's: "What is an author?" Towards a critical discourse of practice as research', in E Barrett & B Bolt (eds.) *Practice as research: Approaches to creative arts inquiry*, I.B. Tauris & Co, London, pp. 135–146.

Barthes, R 1968/1984, 'La mort de l'Auteur', in *Le bruissement de la langue*, Editions du Seuil, Paris, pp. 61–67.

Bassnett, S 1998, *Constructing cultures: Essays on literary translation*, Multilingual Matters, Clevedon.

Beebe, S A 1974, 'Eye contact: a nonverbal determinant of speaker credibility', *The Speech Teacher*, vol. 23, no. 1, pp. 21–25.

Beeby, A 2000, 'Choosing an empirical-experimental model for investigating translation competence', in M Olohan (ed.), *Intercultural faultiness – research models in Translation Studies I – Textual and cognitive aspects*, St Jerome, Manchester, pp. 43–55.

Behr, M 2015, How to back the students – quality, assessment and feedback', in D Andres & M Behr (eds.), *To know how to suggest... Approaches to teaching conference interpreting*, Frank & Timme, Berlin, pp. 201–217.

Bell, S 1997, 'The challenges of setting and monitoring the standards of community interpreting', in S Carr, R Roberts, A Dufour & D Steyn (eds.), *The Critical Link: Interpreters in the community*, John Benjamins, Amsterdam, pp. 93–108.

Biggs, M 2000, 'The foundations of practice-based research: Introduction', *Working papers in art and design*, Vol. 1, University of Hertfordshire, viewed 13 November 2013, http://www.herts.ac.uk/artdes1/research/papers/wpades/vol1/vol1intro.html

Blasco Mayor, M & Amparo, J I 2007, 'E-learning for interpreting', *Babel*, vol. 53, no. 4, pp. 292–302.

Bowen, D & Bowen, M 1989, 'Aptitude for interpreting', in L Gran & J Dodds, (eds.), *The theoretical and practical aspects of teaching conference interpretation*, Campanotto, Udine, pp. 109–125.

Boyle, J 2012, 'Note-taking and secondary students with learning disabilities: challenges and solutions', *Learning Disabilities Research & Practice*, vol. 27, no. 2, pp. 90–10.

Braun, S 2007, 'Interpreting in small-group bilingual videoconferences: challenges and adaptation processes', *Interpreting* vol. 9, no.1, pp. 21–46.

Braun, S 2011, 'Recommendations for the use of video-mediated interpreting in criminal proceedings', in S Braun & J Taylor (eds.), *Videoconference and remote interpreting in criminal proceedings*, Guildford, University of Surrey, pp. 265–287.

Byrne, J 2007, 'Caveat translator: Understanding the legal consequences of errors in professional translation', *The Journal of Specialised Translation*, vol. 7, pp. 2–24.

Calvo, E 2011, 'Translation and/or translator skills as organising principles for curriculum development practice', *The Journal of Specialised Translation*, vol. 16, pp. 5–25.

Camayd-Freixas, E 2005, 'A revolution in consecutive interpretation: Digital Voice-Recorder-Assisted CI', *The ATA Chronicle*, vol. 3, pp. 40–46.

Candy, L 2006, 'Practice-based research: A guide', *CCS Report*, University of Technology, Sydney.

Cardoen, H 2012, 'The effect of note-taking on target text fluency', a CETRA paper, viewed 16 May 2014, http://www.arts.kuleuven.be/cetra/papers/files/cardoen

Centre for Translation Studies University of Vienna (2013): 'About Transcert', viewed 27 December 2013, http://transcert.eu/

Chen, J 2009, 'Authenticity in accreditation tests for interpreters in China', *The Interpreter and Translator Trainer*, vol. 3, no. 2, pp. 257–273.

Chesterman, A &Wagner, E 2002, *Can theory help translators? A dialogue between the ivory tower and the wordface*. St Jerome, Manchester.

Choi, J Y 2006, 'Metacognitive evaluation method in consecutive interpretation for novice learners', *Meta*, vol. 51, no. 2, pp. 273–283.

CIUTI, Conférence internationale permanente d'instituts universitaires de traducteurs et interprètes, viewed 2 October 2013, www.ciuti.org

Clifford, A 2005, 'Putting the exam to the test: Psychometric validation and interpreter certification', *Interpreting*, vol. 7, no. 1, pp. 97–131.

Colbert, E 2009, 'Accommodating the experiential within practice-led research', in *Margins and Mainstreams*, refereed conference papers of the 14th Annual AAWP Conference, viewed 21 October 2014, http://www.aawp.org.au/the_margins_and_mainstreams_papers

Corsellis, A 2008, *Public service interpreting. The first steps*, Palgrave Macmillan, Houndmills.

Cravo, A 2007, 'Action Research in translation Studies', *Journal of Specialised Translation*, vol. 7, pp. 92–107.

Cronin, M 2000, *Across the lines: Travel, language, translation*, Cork University Press, Cork.

Cronin, M 2003, *Translation and globalization*, Routledge, London/New York.

Cronin, M 2010, 'The translation crowd', *Revista Tradumàtica* vol. 8, viewed 2 September 2014, www.fti.uab.es/tradumatica/revista/num8/articles/04/04art.htm

Daryl, H 2013, 'The role of translation education and "Humanities Plus" in liberal education', *Cuadernos de ALDEUU*, vol. 25, pp. 21–35, viewed 21 August 2014, http://aldeeu.org/cuadernos/index.php/CALDEEEU/article/view/33

Dawson, L & Plummer, V 2010, 'Building a system of managing clinical pathways using digital pens', in D Hansen, L Schaper, L & D Rowlands (eds.), *HIC 2010*, vol. 18, pp. 32–36.

De Lemos, M M 2004, 'Effective strategies for the teaching of reading: what works, and why', in B A Knight & W Scott (eds.), *Learning difficulties: Multiple perspectives*, Pearson Education, Frenchs Forest, pp. 17–28.

Delisle, J 1980, *L'Anayse du discours comme méthode de traduction*. Cahiers de traductologie 2, Université d'Ottawa.

De Palma, D, Pielmeier, H, Henderson, S & Stewart, R 2015, The Language Services Market 2015, Common Sense Advisory, Cambridge, Mass. Viewed 17 August 2015, http://www.commonsenseadvisory.com/AbstractView.aspx?ArticleID=26590

Di Vesta, F J & Gray, G S 1973, 'Listening and note-taking II', *Journal of Educational Psychology,* vol. 64, pp. 278–287.

Dollerup, C 1994, 'Systematic feedback in teaching translation' in C Dollerup & A Lindegaard (eds.), *Teaching Translation and Interpreting 2. Insights, Aims, Visions*. John Benjamins, Amsterdam, pp. 121–132.

Dong, D-H & Lan, Y-S 2010, 'Textual competence and the use of cohesion devices in translating into a second language', *The Interpreter and Translator Trainer*, vol. 4, no.1, pp. 47–88.

Drechsel, A 2013, 'Interpreters vs. Technology: Reflections on a difficult relationship', viewed 14 December 2013, https://vkdblog.wordpress.com/tag/ibm/

Drugan, J 2013, *Quality in professional translation*, Bloomsbury, New York.

Echeverri, A 2008, 'Énième plaidoyer pour l'innovation dans les cours pratiques de traduction. Préalables à l'innovation?', *TTR : traduction, terminologie, rédaction*, vol. 21, no. 1, pp. 65–98.

Ellis, L A 2005, *Balancing approaches: revisiting the educational psychology research on teaching students with learning difficulties*, Australian Education Review, ACER, Melbourne.

EMT, the European Master's in Translation, viewed 10 August 2014, www.ec.europa.eu/dgs/translation/programmes/emt/index_en.htm

EMCI, the European Masters in Conference Interpreting, viewed 10 August 2014, www.emcinterpreting.org

Endless Possibilities Talks 2012, 'Technology options for interpreting', viewed 20 March 2013, http://endlesspossibilitiestalks.blogspot.co.uk

Ferrari, M & Hamidi, M 2007, 'Simultaneous consecutive revisited', *SCIC News*, vol. 124, pp. 1–2, viewed 17 September 2013, http://iacovoni.files.wordpress.com/2009/01/simultaneousconsecutive-2.pdf

Ferrari, M 2002, 'Traditional vs. simultaneous consecutive', *SCIC News*, vol. 29, pp. 6–7, viewed 11 May 2013, http://scic.cec.eu.int/scicnews/2002/020130/default_29.htm

Flavell, J H 1979, 'Metacognition and cognitive monitoring', *American Psychologist*, vol. 34, pp. 906–911.

Gabr, M 2007, 'A TQM approach to translator training. Balancing stakeholders' needs and responsibilities', *The Interpreter and Translator Trainer*, vol. 1, no. 1, pp. 65–77.

Gambier, Y & van Doorslaer, L (eds.) 2012, *Handbook of Translation Studies*, vol. 3, John Benjamins, Amsterdam.

Garnham, A 1985, *Psycholinguistics: Central topics*, Routledge, London/New York.

Gentile, A, Ozolins, U & Vasilakakos, M 1996, *Liaison interpreting*, Melbourne University press, Melbourne.

Gile, D 1990, 'Scientific research vs. personal theories in the investigation of interpretation', in L Gran & C Taylor (eds.), *Aspects of applied and experimental research on conference interpretation*, Campanotto, Udine, pp. 28–41.

Gile, D 1991, 'Prise de notes et attention en début d'apprentissage de l'interprétation consécutive – une expérience – démonstration de sensibilisation', *Meta*, vol. 36, no. 2–3, pp. 431–439.

Gile, D 1993, 'The Process-oriented approach in translation training', in C Dollerup & A Lindegaard (eds.), *Teaching translation and interpreting 2*, John Benjamins, Amsterdam/Philadelphia, pp. 107–112.

Gile, D 1995a, *Basic concepts and models for interpreter and translator training*, John Benjamins, Amsterdam.

Gile, D 1995b, 'Interpretation research: A new impetus?', *Hermes, Journal of Linguistics*, vol. 14, pp. 15–29.

Gile, D 2001, 'The role of consecutive in interpreter training: a cognitive view', *Communicate!* September-October, viewed 6 June 2010, http://aiic.net/page/377/the-role-of-consecutive-in-interpreter-training-a-cognitive-view/lang/1

Gile, D 2004, 'Integrated problem and decision reporting as a translator training tool', *The Journal of Specialised Translation*, vol. 2, p. 2–20.

Gile, D 2005, *La traduction, la comprendre, l'apprendre*, Presses Universitaires de France, Paris.

Gile, D 2007, 'A la recherche de la complémentarité de la traduction et l'interprétation en cours de formation à travers des modules théorico-méthodologiques', *Transversalités*, vol. 102, pp. 59–72.

Gile, D 2009a, 'Interpreting Studies: A critical view from within', in A Vidal & J Franco (eds.), *A self-sritical perspective of translation theories*, MONTI, Universidad de Alicante, pp. 135–155.

Gile, D 2009b 'Research for training, research for society in Translation Studies', in A Pym & A Perekrestenko (eds.), *Translation Research Projects 2*. Intercultural Studies Group, Tarragona, pp. 35–40.

Gile, D 2013, Editorial of the CIRIN bulletin, no. 45, p. 2, viewed 14 November 2014, http://www.cirinandgile.com/Bulletin%2045.pdf

Gillies, A 2013, *Conference Interpreting, A Student's Practice Book*, Routledge, London/New York

Goffman, E 1981, *Forms of talk*, University of Pennsylvania Press, Philadelphia.

Gomes, M 2002, 'Digitally mastered consecutive. An interview with Michele Ferrari', *Lingua franca*, vol. 5, no. 6, pp. 6–10, viewed 21 September 2013, http://www.bootheando.com/2008/09/09/consecutiva-simultanea-una-nueva-modalidad-de-interpretacion/

González Davies, M 2004, *Multiple voices in the translation classroom*, John Benjamins, Amsterdam.

Gouadec, D 1989, *Le Traducteur, la traduction et l'entreprise*, AFNOR Gestion, Paris.

Gouadec, D 2002, *Profession: traducteur*, La Maison du Dictionnaire, Paris.

Gouadec, D 2007, *Translation as a Profession*, John Benjamins, Amsterdam/Philadelphia.

Graham, S 2007, 'Learner strategies and self-efficacy: Making the connection', *Language Learning Journal*, vol. 35, pp. 81–93.

Grbic, N 2008, 'Constructing interpreting quality', *Interpreting*, vol. 10, no. 2, pp. 232–257.

Grieve, C R & McGee-Lennon, M R 2010, 'Digitally augmented reminders at home', *Poster presenting results of summer work*, viewed on 14 November 2014, http://www.multimemohome.org/files/papers/PenPosterPortrait_final.pdf

Gu, E & Badler, N I 2006, 'Visual attention and eye gaze during multiparty conversations with distractions', *Intelligent Virtual Agents, Lecture Notes in Computer Science*, vol. 4133, pp. 193–204.

Hale, S & Napier, J 2013, *Research methods in interpreting*, Bloomsbury, London/New York.

Halliday, M A K 2001, 'Towards a theory of good translation', in E Steiner & C Yallop (eds.), *Exploring Translation and Multilingual Text Production*, Mouton de Gruyter, Berlin, pp.307–325.

Hamidi, M 2006, Simultanes Konsekutivdolmetschen. Ein experimenteller Vergleich im Sprachenpaar Französisch-Deutsch, Master thesis, University of Vienna.

Hamidi, M & Pöchhacker, F 2007, 'Simultaneous consecutive interpreting: a new technique put to the test', *Meta*, vol. 52, no. 2, pp. 276–289.

Hansen, I & Shlesinger, M 2007, 'The silver lining. Technology and self-study in the interpreting classroom', *Interpreting*, vol. 9, no. 1, pp. 95–118.

Haseman, B 2006, 'A Manifesto for performative research', *Media International Australia Incorporating Culture and Policy, theme issue "Practice-led Research"*, no. 118, pp. 98–106.

Hatim, B 2001, *Teaching and researching translation*, Pearson Education Limited, Harlow.

Herbert, J 1952, *Manuel de l'interprète*, Librairie de l'Université, Geneva.

Hiebl, B 2011, *Simultanes Konsekutivdolmetschen mit dem LivescribeTM EchoTM Smartpen*, Master thesis, University of Vienna, viewed 20 September 2013, http://othes.univie.ac.at/14608.

Hlavac, J 2013, 'A cross-national overview of translator and interpreter certification procedures', *The International Journal for Translation & Interpreting Research*, vol. 5, no. 1, pp. 32–65.

Holmes, J S 1972/2000, 'The name and nature of Translation Studies', in L Venuti (ed.), *The Translation Studies Reader*, Routledge, London/New York, pp. 180–192

Hönig, H G 1998, 'Positions, power and practice: Functionalist approaches and translation quality assessment', in C Schäffner (ed.), *Translation and quality*. Multilingual Matters, Clevedon, pp. 6–31.

House, J 2014, Translation quality assessment: Past and present', in J House (ed.), *Translation: a multidisciplinary approach*, Palgrave Macmillan, Basingstoke, pp. 241–264.

Hurtado Albir, A (ed.) 1999, *Enseñar a traducir. Metodología en la formación de traductores e intérpretes*, Edelsa, Madrid.

Hurtado Albir, A 2007, 'Competence-based curriculum design for training translators', *The Interpreter and Translator Trainer*, vol. 1, no. 2, pp. 163–195

Ilg, G & Lambert, S 1996, 'Teaching consecutive interpreting', *Interpreting*, vol. 1, no. 1, pp. 69–99.

Interpreting.info. 2012, 'What do you think about simultaneous consecutive?', viewed 15 March 2013, http://interpreting.info/questions/1448/what-do-you-think-about-simultaneous-consecutive.

ISO [International standards organization] 2014, 'ISO 13611: 2014, Interpreting – guidelines for community interpreting', viewed 12 January 2015, https://www.iso.org/obp/ui/#iso:std:iso:13611:ed-1:v1:en

Jones, R 1998, *Conference interpreting explained*, St Jerome, Manchester.

Kalina, S 2002, 'Quality in interpreting and its prerequisites: A framework for a comprehensive view', in G Garzone & M Viezzi (eds.), *Interpreting in the 21st century: challenges and opportunities*, John Benjamins, Amsterdam/Philadelphia, pp. 121–130.

Katan, D 2009a, 'Occupation or profession: A survey of the translators' world', *Translation & Interpreting Studies: The Journal of the American Translation & Interpreting Studies Association*, vol. 4, no. 2, pp. 187– 209.

Katan, D 2009b, 'Translation theory and professional practice: A global survey of the great divide', *Hermes, Journal of Language and Communication Studies*, vol. 42, pp. 111– 153.

Kearns, J 2006, Curriculum renewal in translator training: vocational challenges in academic environments with reference to needs and situation analysis and skills transferability form the contemporary experience of Polish translator training culture, doctoral thesis, Dublin City University, Dublin.

Kearns, J 2008, 'The academic and the vocational in translator education', in J Kearns (ed.), *Translator and interpreter training*, Continuum, London, pp. 185–214.

Kellett Bidoli, C J 2012, 'Interpreting scenarios: Changing modes, ELF and genres' in: C J Kellett Bidoli (ed.), *Interpreting across genres: Multiple research perspectives*, EUT Edizioni Università di Trieste, Trieste, pp. 9–26

Kelly, D 2005, *A handbook for translator trainers*, St Jerome, Manchester.

Kelly, D 2006, 'Adecuación de los sistemas y criterios de evaluación a los objetivos y resultados previstos del aprendizaje en la formación universitaria de traductores', in S Bravo Utrera & R García López (eds.), *Estudios de traducción: Problemas y perspectivas*, ULPGC, Las Palmas de Gran Canaria, pp. 717–729.

Kelly, D 2008, 'Training the trainers: Towards a description of translator trainer competence and training needs analysis', *TTR : traduction, terminologie, rédaction*, vol. 21, no. 1, pp. 99–125.

Kelly, N, Stewart, R G & Hegde, V 2010, *The interpreting marketplace: A study of interpreting in North America commissioned by Interpret America*, Common Sense Advisory, Lowell.

Kiewra, K A 1989, 'A review of note-taking: the encoding storage paradigm and beyond', *Educational Psychology Review*, vol. 1, pp. 147–172.

Kiewra, K A, & Benton, S L 1988, 'The relationship between information-processing ability and note-taking', *Contemporary Educational Psychology*, vol. 13, pp. 33–44.

Kiraly, D 1995, 'Pathways to translation: pedagogy and process', *Translation Studies*, vol. 3, Kent State University Press, Kent.

Kiraly, D 2000, *A social constructivist approach to translator education: Empowerment from theory to practice*, St Jerome, Manchester.

Kurz, I 2001, 'Conference interpreting: Quality in the ears of the user', *Meta*, vol. 45, no. 2, pp. 394–409.

Lambert, S 1988, 'A human information processing and cognitive approach to the training of simultaneous interpreters', in D L Hammond (ed.), *Language at crossroads. Proceedings of the 29th annual conference of the ATA*, Learned Information, Medford, pp. 379–387.

Lambert, W E 1978, 'Psychological approaches to bilingualism, translation and interpretation', in D Gerver & H Sinaiko (eds.), *Language, interpretation and communication*, Plenum Press, New York, pp. 131–143.

Larose, R 1998, 'Méthodologie de l'évaluation des traductions', *Meta*, vol. 43, no. 2, pp. 163–86.

Lindquist, P P 2005, 'Technologies, discourse analysis, and the spoken word: the MRC approach, an empirical approach to interpreter performance evaluation and pedagogy', *Meta*, vol. 50, no. 4, doi: 10.7202/019848ar

Lindstrom, J H 2007, 'Determining appropriate accommodations for postsecondary students with reading and written expression disorders', *Learning Disabilities Research & Practice*, vol. 22, no. 4, pp. 229–236.

Lombardi, J 2003, 'DRAC Interpreting: Coming soon to a courthouse near you?', *Proteus*, vol. 12, no. 2, pp. 7–9, viewed 12 March 2013, http://www.najit.org/proteus/PDFVersions/Proteus_Spr03%20web.pdf

Lörscher, W 1992, 'Process-oriented research into translation and implications for translation teaching', *TTR: traduction, terminologie, redaction*, vol. 5, no. 1, pp. 145–161.

Maier, C 2007, 'The translator's visibility: the rights and responsibilities thereof', in M Salama-Carr, (ed.), *Translating and Interpreting Conflict*, Rodopi, Amsterdam/New York, pp. 253–266.

Marco, J 2004, '¿Tareas o proyectos? ¿Senderos que se bifurcan en el desarrollo de la competencia traductora?', *Trans*, vol. 8, pp. 75–88.

Martínez Melis, N & Hurtado Albir, A 2001, 'Assessment in translation studies: research needs', *Meta*, vol. 46, no. 2, pp. 272–287.

Mead, P 2000, 'Control of pauses by trainee interpreters in their A and B languages', *The Interpreters' Newsletter*, vol. 10, pp. 89–102.

Mead, P 2012, 'Consecutive interpreting at a literature festival', in C J Kellett Bidoli (ed.), *Interpreting across genres: Multiple research perspectives*, EUT Edizioni, Università di Trieste, Trieste, pp. 171–183.

Mikkelson, H 2013, 'Universities and interpreter certification', *The International Journal of Translation and Interpreting Research*, vol 5, no. 1, pp. 66–78.

Mikkelson, H & Mintz, H 1997, 'Orientation workshops for interpreters of all languages: How to strike a balance between the ideal world and reality', in S Carr, R Roberts, A Dufour & D Steyn (eds.), *The Critical Link: Interpreters in the Community*, John Benjamins, Amsterdam/Philadelphia, pp. 55–64.

Moser-Mercer, B 2005, 'Remote interpreting: issues of multi-sensory integration in a multilingual task', *Meta*, vol. 50, no. 2, pp. 727–738.

Mossop, B 2001, *Revising and editing for translators*, St Jerome, Manchester.

NAATI, the National Accreditation Authority for Translators and Interpreters, Australia, viewed 17 August 2013, www.naati.com.au

Napier, J 2011, 'Here or there? An assessment of video remote signed language interpreter-mediated interaction in court' in S Braun & J Taylor (eds.), *Videoconference and remote interpreting in criminal proceedings*, University of Surrey, Guildford, pp. 145–185.

Navarro-Hall, E 2012, 'An introduction to sim-consec', viewed 19 April 2013, http://1culture.net/1culture/anintroduction-to-sim-consec.

Neff, J 2015, 'Professionalisation: A systematic didactic approach, in D Andres & M Behr (eds.), *To know how to suggest... Approaches to teaching conference interpreting*, Frank & Timme, Berlin, pp. 219–242.

Nelson, R (ed.) 2013, *Practice as research in the arts: Principles, protocols, pedagogies, resistances*, Palgrave Macmillan, Basingstoke.

Neves, J 2005, 'We do not teach translation, we train translators: An interview with Yves Gambier', *Translating Today*, vol. 2, pp. 23–25.

Niska, H 2005, 'Training interpreters. Programmes, curricula, practices', in M Tennent (ed.), *Training for the New Millenium. Pedagogies for translation and interpreting*, John Benjamins, Amsterdam/Philadelphia, pp. 35–64.

Nolan, J (2012), *Interpretation: Techniques and exercises (2nd ed.)*, Multilingual matters, Clevedon.

Nord, C 1991, *Text analysis in translation*, trans. C Nord & P Sparrow, Rodopi, Amsterdam.

Nord, C 1997, *Translating as a purposeful activity. Functionalist approaches explained*, St. Jerome, Manchester.

Orlando, M 2010a, 'Interpreting eloquence: when words matter as much as ideas', *The AALITRA Review: a Journal of Literary Translation*, vol. 1, pp. 52–60.

Orlando, M 2010b, 'Digital pen technology and consecutive interpreting: Another dimension in note-taking training and assessment'. *The Interpreters' Newsletter*, vol. 15, pp. 71–86.

Orlando, M 2011, 'Evaluations of translations in the training of professional translators: At the crossroads between theoretical, professional and pedagogical practices', *The Interpreter and Translator Trainer*, vol. 5, no. 2, pp. 293–308.

Orlando, M 2014, 'A study on the amenability of digital pen technology in a hybrid mode of interpreting: Consec-simul with notes', *The International Journal of Translation and Interpreting Research*, vol. 6, no. 2, pp. 39–54.

Orlando, M 2015a, 'Digital pen technology and interpreter training, practice and research: Status and trends' in S Ehrlich & J Napier (eds.), *Interpreter Education in the Digital Age*, Gallaudet University Press, Washington DC, pp. 125–152.

Orlando, M 2015b, 'Implementing digital pen technology in the consecutive interpreting classroom', in D Andres & M Behr (eds.), *To Know how to Suggest... Approaches to teaching Conference Interpreting*, Frank & Timme, Berlin, pp. 171–199.

Ozolins, U 2011, 'Telephone interpreting: understanding practice and identifying research needs', *The International Journal of Translation and Interpreting Research*, vol. 3, no. 2. pp. 33–47.

Perez-Guarneri, V & Ziegler, K (Interview with) 2013, ISO Standards on Interpreting, *The AIIC Webzine,* viewed 23 November 2014, http://aiic.net/page/6648/iso-standards-on-interpreting/lang/1

Pöchhacker, F 2002, 'Researching interpreting quality: models and methods', in G Garzone & M Viezzi (eds.), *Interpreting in the 21st century: challenges and opportunities*, John Benjamins, Amsterdam and Philadelphia, pp. 95–106.

Pöchhacker, F 2004, *Introducing Interpreting Studies.* Routledge, London/New York.

Pöchhacker, F 2010, 'The role of research in interpreter education', *The International Journal for Translation & Interpreting Research, vol. 2, pp.* 1–10.

Pöchhacker, F 2012, *Consecutive 2.0,* Paper presented at the 53rd annual conference of the ATA, San Diego.

Pokorn, N & Koskinen, K (eds.) 2013, *New horizons in translation research and education*, vol 1, University of Eastern Finland, viewed 11 December 2014, http://www.academia.edu/6019983/Assessment_Feedback_in_Translator_Training_A_Dual_Perspective

Pym, A 2003, 'Redefining translation competence in an electronic age. In defence of a minimalist approach', *Meta*, vol. 48, no. 4, pp. 481–497.

Pym, A 2005, 'Training translators – ten recurrent naiveties', *Translating Today*, vol. 2, pp. 3–6.

Pym, A 2006, 'Localization, training and the threat of fragmentation', viewed 23 November 2014, http://usuaris.tinet.cat/apym/on-line/translation/translation.html

Pym, A 2010a, *Exploring translation theories*, Routledge, London/New York.

Pym, A 2010b, 'Translation theory today and tomorrow – Responses to equivalence', in L N Zybatow (ed.), *Translationswissenschaft – Stand und Perspektiven*, Peter Lang, Frankfurt, pp. 1–14.

Pym, A, Grin, F, Sfreddo, C & Chan, A L J 2012, *The status of the translation profession in the European Union*, European Commission, Luxembourg, viewed 12 September 2013, http://ec.europa.eu/dgs/translation/publications/studies/translation_profession_en.pdf

Pym, A & Torres-Simón, E 2014, 'The professional backgrounds of translation scholars', *Report on a survey*, Intercultural Studies Group, Universitat Rovira i Virgili, viewed 3 October 2014, http://usuaris.tinet.cat/apym/online/research_methods/2014_ESTsurvey_article.pdf

Quah, C K 2006, *Translation and technology*, Palgrave Macmillan, Basingstoke.

Rivers, W P 2001, 'Autonomy at all costs: an ethnography of metacognitive self-assessment and self-management among experienced language learners', *The modern language journal*, vol. 85, no. 2, pp. 279–290.

Rozan, J-F 1956, *La Prise de notes dans l'interprétation consécutive*, Librairie de l'Université, Geneva.

Şahin, M & Dungan, N 2014, 'Translation testing and evaluation: A study on methods and needs', *The International Journal of Translation and Interpreting Research*, vol. 6, no. 2, pp. 67–90.

Sandrelli, A 2012, 'Computer Assisted Interpreter Training 15 years on: Main achievements and future challenges', *Exploiting emerging technologies to prepare interpreters and their clients for professional practice*, YVY seminar, viewed 14 November 2013, http://www.virtual-interpreting.net/assets/IVY-Symposium-Presentations/IVY-Dissemination-Booklet.pdf

Sawyer, D B 2004, *Fundamental aspects of interpreter education: Curriculum and assessment*, John Benjamins, Amsterdam/Philadelphia.

Schäffner, C 1997a, 'From 'good' to 'functionally appropriate': assessing translation quality', *Current Issues in Language and Society*, vol. 4, no. 1, pp. 1–5.

Schäffner, C 1997b, 'Skopos theory', in M Baker (ed.), *Encyclopedia of Translation Studies*, Routledge, London.

Scriven, M 1967, 'The methodology of evaluation', *Perspectives of Curriculum Evaluation*, vol. 1, pp. 39–55.

Seleskovitch, D 1968, *L'interprète dans les conférences internationales: problèmes de langage et de communication*, Minard, Paris.

Seleskovitch, D 1975, *Langage, langues et mémoire. Etude de la prise de notes en interprétation consécutive*, Minard, Paris.

Seleskovitch, D 1976, Interpretation, a psychological approach to translating, in R W Brislin (ed.), *Translation: applications and research*, Gardiner, New York, pp. 92–116.

Seleskovitch, D 1978, *Interpreting for international conferences*, Pen and Booth, Washington, D. C.

Seleskovitch, D & Lederer, M 1984/2001, *Interpréter pour traduire*, Didier Erudition, Paris.

Seleskovitch, D & Lederer, M 1989, *Pédagogie raisonnée de l'interprétation*, OPOCE/ Didier Erudition, Bruxelles/Luxembourg.

Setton, R 1999, *Simultaneous interpretation: A cognitive-pragmatic analysis*, John Benjamins, Amsterdam/Philadelphia.

Setton, R 2010, 'From practice to theory and back in interpreting: the pivotal role of training', *The Interpreters' Newsletter*, vol. 15, pp. 1–18

Shlesinger, M 1995, 'Strangers in paradigms: What lies ahead for simultaneous interpreting research?', *Target*, vol. 7, no. 1, pp. 7–28.

Shlesinger, M 2009, 'Crossing the divide: What researchers and practitioners can learn from one another', *The international journal for translation and interpreting research*, vol.1, no. 1, pp. 1–16.

Snell-Hornby, M 2006, *The turns of Translation Studies: New paradigms or shifting viewpoints?*, John Benjamins, Amsterdam/Philadelphia.

Spivak, G 2000, 'The Politics of translation', in L Venuti (ed.), *The Translation Studies Reader*, Routledge, London, pp. 397–416.

Stejskal, J 2005, *Survey of the FIT committee for information on the status of the translation & interpretation profession*, International Federation of Translators, Geneva.

Tran, T A T & Lawson, M 2001, 'Students' procedures for reviewing lecture notes', *International Education Journal: Educational Research Conference 2001*, vol. 2, no. 4, pp. 278–293.

U.S. Bureau of Labor Statistics, Occupational Outlook Handbook, viewed 17 August 2015, http://www.bls.gov/ooh/media-and-communication/interpreters-and-translators.htm

van Hoof, H 1962, *Théorie et pratique de l'interprétation*, Max Hueber, Munich.

Veenman, M V J 2006, 'Metacognition and learning: conceptual and methodological considerations', *Metacognition and Learning*, vol. 1, pp. 3–14.

Vienne, J 1994, 'Pour une pédagogie de la traduction en situation', in M Snell-Hornby, F Pöchhacker & K Kaindl (eds.), *Translation Studies – an interdiscipline*, John Benjamins, Amsterdam, pp. 421–431.

Vivas, J 2003, 'Simultaneous Consecutive, Report on the comparison session of June 11, 2003', *SCIC B4/JV D2003*, Joint Interpreting and Service, European Commission, Brussels.

Wadensjö, C 2011, 'Interpreting in theory and practice: reflections about an alleged gap, in C Alvstad, A Hild, E Tiselius (eds.), *Methods and strategies of process research: integrative approaches in Translation Studies*, John Benjamins, Amsterdam, pp. 13–21.

Wasbourne, K 2014, 'Beyond error marking: written corrective feedback for a dialogic pedagogy in translator training', *The Interpreter and Translator Trainer*, vol. 8, no. 2, pp. 240–256.

Way, C 2006, 'Evaluación efectiva: el talón de Aquiles', in S Bravo Utrera & R García López (eds.), *Estudios de traducción: problemas y perspectivas*, ULPGC, Las Palmas de Gran Canaria , pp. 755–762.

Way, C 2008, 'Systematic assessment of translator competence: in search of Achilles' heel', in J Kearns (ed.), *Translator and interpreter training*, Continuum, London, pp. 88–103.

Websites for Translators, 2012, 'Technology-assisted interpreting? Why not!', viewed 20 March 2013, http://websitesfortranslators.co.uk/webdesign/blog/technology-assisted-interpreting-why-not.

Wenden, A L 1999, 'An introduction to metacognitive knowledge and beliefs in language learning: beyond the basics', *System*, vol. 27, pp. 435–441

Wetswood, P 2008, *What teachers need to know about teaching methods*, ACER Press, Camberwell.

Winteringham, S 2010, 'The usefulness of ICTs in interpreting practice', *The Interpreters' Newsletter*, vol. 15, pp. 87–99.

Yates, G C R & Yates, S 1990, 'Teacher-effectiveness research: towards describing user-friendly classroom instruction', *Educational Psychology*, vol.10, no. 3, pp. 253–265.

Zwischenberger, C 2013, *Qualität und Rollenbilder beim simultanen Konferenzdolmetschen*, Frank & Timme, Berlin.

Zwischenberger, C & Behr, M 2015, *Interpreting quality: A look around and ahead*, Frank & Timme, Berlin.

#IntJC The Interpreting Journal Club, 2012, 'Digital pen and note-taking', Session 17, 06/09/2012, viewed on 12 April 2013, https://sites.google.com/site/interpretjc/home/archive.

TRANSKULTURALITÄT – TRANSLATION – TRANSFER

Bd. 1   Cornelia Zwischenberger: Qualität und Rollenbilder beim simultanen Konferenzdolmetschen. 434 Seiten. ISBN 978-3-86596-527-1

Bd. 2   Sarah Fünfer: Mensch oder Maschine? Dolmetscher und maschinelles Dolmetschsystem im Vergleich. 150 Seiten. ISBN 978-386596-548-6

Bd. 3   Dörte Andres/Martina Behr (Hg.): Die Wahrheit, die reine Wahrheit und nichts als die Wahrheit. Erinnerungen der russischen Dolmetscherin Tatjana Stupnikova an den Nürnberger Prozess. 242 Seiten. ISBN 978-3-7329-0005-3

Bd. 4   Larisa Schippel (Hg.): Magda Jeanrenaud: Universalien des Übersetzens. 332 Seiten. ISBN 978-3-86596-444-1

Bd. 5   Sylvia Reinart: Lost in Translation (Criticism)? Auf dem Weg zu einer konstruktiven Übersetzungskritik. 438 Seiten. ISBN 978-3-7329-0014-5

Bd. 6   Sophia Scherl: Die deutsche Übersetzungskultur in der zweiten Hälfte des 18. Jahrhunderts. Meta Forkel-Liebeskind und ihre Übersetzung der *Rights of Man*. 152 Seiten. ISBN 978-3-7329-0020-6

Bd. 7   Thomas Kammer: Basiswissen für Dolmetscher – Deutschland und Spanien. 204 Seiten. ISBN 978-3-7329-0035-0

Bd. 8   Dorothee Jacobs: Basiswissen für Dolmetscher – Deutschland und das Vereinigte Königreich Großbritannien und Nordirland. 192 Seiten. ISBN 978-3-7329-0036-7

Bd. 9   Sophia Roessler: Basiswissen für Dolmetscher – Deutschland und Italien. 212 Seiten. ISBN 978-3-7329-0039-8

Bd. 10 Annika Selnow: Basiswissen für Dolmetscher – Deutschland und Frankreich. 192 Seiten. ISBN 978-3-7329-0040-4

Bd. 12 Alice Leal: Is the Glass Half Empty or Half Full? Reflections on Translation Theory and Practice in Brazil. 334 Seiten. ISBN 978-3-7329-0068-8

Bd. 13 Kristina Werner: Zwischen Neutralität und Propaganda – Französisch-Dolmetscher im Nationalsozialismus. 130 Seiten. ISBN 978-3-7329-0085-5

Bd. 14 Larisa Schippel/Magda Jeanrenaud/Julia Richter (Hg.): „Traducerile au de cuget să îmblînzească obiceiurile …". Rumänische Übersetzungsgeschichte – Prozesse, Produkte, Akteure. 368 Seiten. ISBN 978-3-7329-0087-9

Bd. 15 Elena Kalašnikova (Hg.): „Übersetzer sind die Wechselpferde der Aufklärung". Im Gespräch: Russische Übersetzerinnen und Übersetzer deutscher Literatur. 254 Seiten. ISBN 978-3-7329-0097-8

Frank & Timme

TRANSKULTURALITÄT – TRANSLATION – TRANSFER

Bd. 16   Dörte Andres/Martina Behr (eds.): To Know How to Suggest … Approaches to Teaching Conference Interpreting. 260 Seiten. ISBN 978-3-7329-0114-2

Bd. 17   Tatiana Bedson/Maxim Schulz: Sowjetische Übersetzungskultur in den 1920er und 1930er Jahren. Die Verlage *Vsemirnaja literatura* und *Academia*. 182 Seiten. ISBN 978-3-7329-0142-5

Bd. 18   Cécile Balbous: Das Sprachknaben-Institut der Habsburgermonarchie in Konstantinopel. 90 Seiten. ISBN 978-3-7329-0149-4

Bd. 19   Cornelia Zwischenberger/Martina Behr (eds.): Interpreting Quality: A Look Around and Ahead. 334 Seiten. ISBN 978-3-7329-0191-3

Bd. 20   Mehmet Tahir Öncü: Basiswissen für Dolmetscher – Deutschland und die Türkei. 232 Seiten. ISBN 978-3-7329-0154-8

Bd. 21   Marc Orlando: Training 21st century translators and interpreters: At the crossroads of practice, research and pedagogy. 158 Seiten. ISBN 978-3-7329-0245-3

Bd. 22   Christian Trollmann: Nationalsozialismus auf Japanisch? Deutsch-japanische Beziehungen 1933–1945 aus translationssoziologischer Sicht. 154 Seiten. ISBN 978-3-7329-0281-1

Bd. 23   Ursula Gross-Dinter (Hg.): Dolmetschen 3.0 – Einblicke in einen Beruf im Wandel. 226 Seiten. ISBN 978-3-7329-0188-3

Bd. 24   Lieven D'hulst/Carol O'Sullivan/Michael Schreiber (eds.): Politics, Policy and Power in Translation History. 256 Seiten. ISBN 978-3-7329-0173-9

Bd. 25   Dörte Andres/Julia Richter/Larisa Schippel (Hg.): Translation und „Drittes Reich". Menschen – Entscheidungen – Folgen. 352 Seiten. ISBN 978-3-7329-0302-3

Bd. 26   Julia Richter/Cornelia Zwischenberger/Stefanie Kremmel/Karlheinz Spitzl (Hg.): (Neu-)Kompositionen. Aspekte transkultureller Translationswissenschaft. 404 Seiten. ISBN 978-3-7329-0306-1

Bd. 27   Barbara den Ouden: Translation und Emotion: Untersuchung einer besonderen Komponente des Dolmetschens. 438 Seiten. ISBN 978-3-7329-0304-7

Bd. 28   Larisa Schippel/Cornelia Zwischenberger (eds.): Going East: Discovering New and Alternative Traditions in Translation Studies. 540 Seiten. ISBN 978-3-7329-0335-1

Bd. 29   Dörte Andres/Klaus Kaindl/Ingrid Kurz (Hg.): Dolmetscherinnen und Dolmetscher im Netz der Macht. Autobiographisch konstruierte Lebenswege in autoritären Regimen. 280 Seiten. ISBN 978-3-7329-0336-8

Frank & Timme

TRANSKULTURALITÄT – TRANSLATION – TRANSFER

Bd. 30 Martina Behr/Sabine Seubert (Hg.): Education is a Whole-Person Process. Von ganzheitlicher Lehre, Dolmetschforschung und anderen Dingen. 516 Seiten. ISBN 978-3-7329-0324-5

Bd. 31 Simone Kellner: Basiswissen für Dolmetscher und Übersetzer – Österreich. 108 Seiten. ISBN 978-3-7329-0370-2

Bd. 32 Simon Zupan/Aleksandra Nuč (eds.): Interpreting Studies at the Crossroads of Disciplines. 204 Seiten. ISBN 978-3-7329-0045-9

Bd. 33 Hilke Effinghausen: Zwischen Neutralität und Propaganda – Spanisch-Dolmetscher im Nationalsozialismus. 178 Seiten. ISBN 978-3-7329-0394-8

Bd. 34 Lars Felgner: Nonverbale Kommunikation beim medizinischen Dolmetschen. 428 Seiten. ISBN 978-3-7329-0386-3

Bd. 35 Annika Schlesiger: Berufsschutz für Übersetzer und Dolmetscher in Deutschland. Vergangenheit – Gegenwart – und Zukunft? 200 Seiten. ISBN 978-3-7329-0408-2

Bd. 36 Lena Skalweit: Dolmetscher und ihre Ausbildung im Zeitalter der europäischen Expansion. Osmanisches Reich und Afrika. 312 Seiten. ISBN 978-3-7329-0371-9

Bd. 37 Samantha Blai: Basiswissen für Dolmetscher und Übersetzer – Deutschland und Polen. 306 Seiten. ISBN 978-3-7329-0446-4

Bd. 38 Jette Knapp: Basiswissen für Dolmetscher und Übersetzer – Deutschland und USA. 248 Seiten. ISBN 978-3-7329-0447-1

Bd. 39 Thomas Baumgart/Mona Gerlach: Basiswissen für Dolmetscher und Übersetzer – Deutschland und Spanien. 254 Seiten. ISBN 978-3-7329-0465-5

Bd. 40 Amrei Bahr/Katja Hagedorn: Basiswissen für Dolmetscher und Übersetzer – Deutschland und das Vereinigte Königreich Großbritannien und Nordirland. 236 Seiten. ISBN 978-3-7329-0467-9

Bd. 41 Saskia Isabelle Riemke/Eleonora Pepe: Basiswissen für Dolmetscher und Übersetzer – Deutschland und Italien. 276 Seiten. ISBN 978-3-7329-0468-6

Bd. 42 Miriam Heike Schroers: Basiswissen für Dolmetscher und Übersetzer – Deutschland und Frankreich. 280 Seiten. ISBN 978-3-7329-0485-3

Bd. 43 Charlotte P. Kieslich: Dolmetschen im Nationalsozialismus. Die Reichsfachschaft für das Dolmetscherwesen (RfD). 428 Seiten. ISBN 978-3-7329-0515-7

Bd. 44 Viktoria Fedorovskaja/Tatiana Yudina: Basiswissen für Dolmetscher und Übersetzer – Deutschland und Russland. 264 Seiten. ISBN 978-3-7329-0487-7

F Frank & Timme

TRANSKULTURALITÄT – TRANSLATION – TRANSFER

Bd. 45   Ke Liu: Basiswissen für Dolmetscher und Übersetzer – Deutschland und China.
228 Seiten. ISBN 978-3-7329-0527-0

Bd. 46   Antonina Lakner: Peter de Mendelssohn – Translation, Identität und Exil.
414 Seiten. ISBN 978-3-7329-0491-4

Bd. 47   Sabine Seubert: Visuelle Informationen beim Simultandolmetschen.
Eine Eyetracking-Studie. 402 Seiten. ISBN 978-3-7329-0572-0

Bd. 48   Kimberly Dinnissen/Rob Soons: Basiswissen für Dolmetscher und Übersetzer –
Deutschland und die Niederlande. 270 Seiten. ISBN 978-3-7329-0583-6

Bd. 49   Martina Behr: Dolmetschen: Komplexität, Methodik, Modellierung.
288 Seiten. ISBN 978-3-7329-0635-2

Bd. 50   Aleksey Tashinskiy/Julija Boguna/Andreas F. Kelletat (Hg.):
Übersetzer und Übersetzen in der DDR. Translationshistorische Studien.
292 Seiten. ISBN 978-3-7329-0698-7

Bd. 51   Kate Reiserer: Vier Übersetzerinnen und ihre neun Ehemänner.
Ehe und Übersetzung in der Romantik. 154 Seiten. ISBN 978-3-7329-0755-7

Bd. 52   Larisa Schippel/Julia Richter (Hg.): Translation und „Drittes Reich".
Translationsgeschichte als methodologische Herausforderung. 370 Seiten.
ISBN 978-3-7329-0661-1

Bd. 53   Aleksey Tashinskiy/Julija Boguna/Tomasz Rozmysłowicz (Hg.):
Translation und Exil (1933–1945) I. Namen und Orte. Recherchen zur Geschichte
des Übersetzens. 494 Seiten. ISBN 978-3-7329-0744-1

Bd. 54   Hildegard Maria Mader: Von Paris nach Kairo: Wissenstransfer im *Paris-Bericht*
Rifā'a Rāfi' aṭ-Ṭahṭāwīs. Ein Beitrag zur Übersetzungsgeschichte Ägyptens
im 19. Jahrhundert. 118 Seiten. ISBN 978-3-7329-0841-7

Bd. 55   Yafen Zhao: Take it or leave it? Notationstechnik beim Konsekutivdolmetschen
Chinesisch–Deutsch. 276 Seiten. ISBN 978-3-7329-0871-4

Bd. 56   Hannah Spannring: Lore Segal – Ein translatorisches Porträt im Kontext Exil.
238 Seiten. ISBN 978-3-7329-0901-8